UNITED
~~TES~~

MEXICO

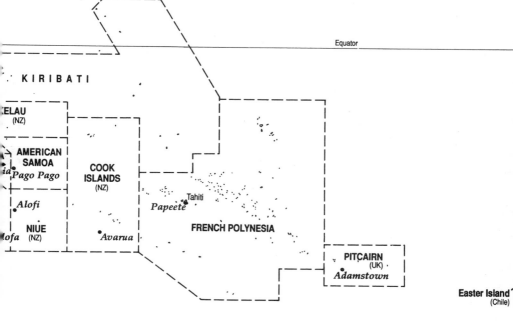

HAWAIIAN ISLANDS (USA)

Kauai

Oahu

Honolulu • Maui

Hilo

Hawaii

I F I C   O C E A N

Equator

K I R I B A T I

~~ELAU~~
(NZ)

**AMERICAN
SAMOA**

ia Pago Pago

Alofi

NIUE
(NZ)

ofa

**COOK
ISLANDS**
(NZ)

Papeete Tahiti

Avarua

FRENCH POLYNESIA

PITCAIRN
(UK)

Adamstown

Easter Island
(Chile)

PACIFIC
ODYSSEY

PACIFIC ODYSSEY

The islands of the South Seas

Cherry Farrow

MICHAEL O'MARA BOOKS LIMITED

First published in Great Britain in 1990 by
Michael O'Mara Books Limited
9 Lion Yard
11–13 Tremadoc Road
London SW4 7NF

A CIP catalogue record for this book is available
from the British Library

ISBN 1–85479–010–2

Designed by Richard Souper
Typeset by Florencetype Limited, Kewstoke, Avon
Printed and bound in Great Britain by
Redwood Press Limited, Melksham, Wiltshire

CONTENTS

INTRODUCTION
A Vanishing Paradise
7

PAPUA NEW GUINEA
At the End of the Rainbow
13

TAHITI
Another Side of Paradise
59

HAWAII
Disney Comes to Paradise
87

PALAU
Troubles in Paradise
118

WESTERN SAMOA
The Last Earthly Paradise
138

AMERICAN SAMOA
Roads to Nowhere
170

NOTES
175

Illustration Acknowledgements

The Publishers gratefully acknowledge permission to reproduce the pictures on the following pages:

D. Ball/Spectrum Colour Library: opposite p.96; between pp.96–7 left

Cherry Farrow: opposite p.32; between pp.32–3; between pp.64–5; opposite p.65; opposite p.97

C.B. and D.W. Frith/Bruce Coleman Limited: opposite p.113 above

Patricio Goycolea/Hutchinson Library: between pp.112–3 top right

Michael MacIntyre/Hutchinson Library: between pp.96–7 right; opposite p.112; between pp.112–3 left and bottom right; opposite p.113 below

M.A. MacKenzie: opposite p.33; opposite p.64

Endpapers: Richard Natkiel Associates

INTRODUCTION
A VANISHING PARADISE

Papua New Guinea's most famous son, the poet John Kasaipolowa, wrote an epic three-part poem based on a story from the Trobriand islands. 'Sail the Midnight Sun' was to become very famous, and was even performed at the Edinburgh Festival. It tells of the origins of Papua New Guinea, born of a union between the sun and the sea. Niugini, the hero, is the envy of men and the target of women. He hears of a beautiful woman in the east and leaves the place of his childhood. He progresses through maturity, the struggle for independence, marriage, the experience of independence and the reality of independence. The storm of life is severe – so severe that Niugini is forced to call for all those things which once had meaning in his life. The only response is silence. There is no response. He is lost.

★

On melancholy days I used to climb a dirt road that wound through gardens of cane high above Papua New Guinea's capital, Port Moresby, to watch the sun go down, an impossible gold sinking into a black sea until only the reflections in the sky remained, surrealistic as only a tropical sunset can be. It seemed never enough to be living on one island in the Pacific – I wanted to know what lay beyond the rim of the ocean, what the islands on the other side looked like.

At a festival in Moresby I had my first glimpse of Polynesians – Tahitians and other islanders, Kiribati and Tuvaluans. They were very different from Papua New Guineans, who, anyway, were all different from each other. I was mesmerized by the grace of the Tahitians and awe-struck by the size and speed of the Solomon Islanders paddling their great war-canoes.

My Pacific wanderlust became acute and I fantasized of sailing beyond Moresby's reef and into the 'real' Pacific. Papua New Guinea was a twentieth-century land of Toyota Land Cruisers and entrepreneurs, cowboys. For too long I was unable to leave the capital. I longed to get out. Though even Port Moresby had its compensations. On my drive to work the great mountains of the Owen Stanley Range loomed in the distance, grey and purple through the morning heat haze, while a twenty-minute drive in the other direction took me past the lagoon, dotted with lush, velvet-green islets. After the rainy season was over, these looked more like large rocks as they turned to scrub-brown dirt. There were markets and flame-trees and African tulip-trees and woven houses that rose on stilts out of the lagoon where, in the early morning, wood-smoke rose and children fished. At night, vivid green tree-frogs languished under the porch light, waiting to attack the mosquitoes. I used to hold my breath with the strangeness and beauty of it all, although I never felt a part of it.

When I first escaped from Port Moresby, I began to understand what everyone had been on about. In Papua New Guinea's Highlands, I drove up the Highlands Highway, a yellow dirt road that starts in flat, tropical bush country and then crosses the plain that is the Markham Valley before climbing into the Eastern Highlands. In the early mornings we drove through and above low-hanging cloud and past canopies of trees with broad, yellow flowers towards Mount Wilhelm and the Waghi Valley. The village huts were round and woven. At Wabag the highway took on an almost Mediterranean look, lined with casuarina trees, and that night I showered under a perforated bucket of warm water, at the same time gazing over a flimsy bathroom wall woven from pandanus to valleys and mountains that stretched far into the horizon. The mountain ranges and valleys worked their magic in the same way that the ocean did. There still had to be something even more magical beyond them.

My first visit out of Papua New Guinea itself was to the Solomon Islands. Somewhere across the Solomon Sea, palm trees and golden sands emerged from the blue sea below us. The tiny plane landed on a grass landing-strip lined with bush and jungle and taxied to a halt in front of large corrugated-iron building, bent to an eggshell shape. Over the gap which formed the doorway, faded lettering announced 'Munda International Airport'. Now, for the first time, I felt truly in the South Seas. When we finally landed on Guadalcanal, the major island in the Solomons, I walked into the capital, Honiara, and in the main street saw real convicts in white pyjama uniforms with arrows on them, mowing the lawns and weeding the gardens in front of the law courts.

Guadalcanal no longer resounded to the sounds of battle or tanks or John Wayne but to the sound of the sea crashing on to the reef, a guitar being played softly through the night, the chatter of mynah birds and a fresh carpet of frangipani flowers under the trees in the mornings. This really was the Pacific, and very different to the urban sprawl of Port Moresby. So different that, when we flew back to Jackson's Airport and approached Moresby, the captain of the plane turned the cabin lights off so that we might see the bright lights clearly below. There weren't many, but he was rewarded by the ooghs and aaghs from those of us who had come from the remoter islands of the South Seas!

Alan Moorehead's *Fatal Impact*[1] started a century earlier, long before the age of air travel. Now it was unstoppable it seemed. Pacific paradises were racing into the twenty-first century. The New Hebrides, a condominium of islands, administered jointly by Britain and France, broke loose and waged a mini-revolution, seeking self-rule, which it got. It also got a new name, Vanuatu. The first rumblings of separatism were being heard in New Caledonia, France's nickel-rich island in Melanesia. Papua New Guinea too, though independent, was experiencing violence and alienation in its cities. Bougainville, its easternmost island, had long wanted to secede and become part of the Solomons. In the North Pacific, Micronesian islands, for years a direct and crucial part of the American military system, were debating their future status as an American colony or whether they could go it alone. Abject poverty was leading many of the small islands to make pacts with various devils – the military, tourism, logging companies. The future for the islands is unclear depending on the dollar and the yen, the whims of businessmen and governments.

I realized during the too brief time I was living there how little I knew of those other islands and cultures and how different it all was to the dreams of 'the last earthly paradise'. If there was an earthly paradise, and some of the islands certainly came near it, then it was for white men – and I use 'men' deliberately – not for the islanders themselves, who had been robbed, exploited and brutalized over many years. The realities were and are, gold before coconuts, oil before fishing rights, and nuclear weapons before human rights.

Although I saw the realities at the time and understood them, I didn't entirely accept them myself. There was always some small island, some small Pacific town that promised more – an earthly paradise to be discovered or rediscovered. And so I decided to make my own journey, and ended up making three. It took me three long journeys, each one over many months, to research this book that I suppose I hoped would lead me to my own unspoilt island. I touched upon only half a dozen or so out of twenty-five thousand or more Pacific islands and found upon each return journey that I was out of date again. Papua New Guinea's potential riches had catapulted it into a kind of lawless Wild West, where a good many of the Europeans now carried guns and there were no sheriffs to speak of. As uncontrolled tribal fighting in Papua New Guinea's Western Highlands entered its sixth month, a former Prime Minister together with forty other MPs was accused of misconduct and misappropriation of shares in a mining share flotation.

In Bougainville, after almost two years of guerrilla fighting, the great Panguna copper mine, Papua New Guinea's main source of revenue, closed down. In Micronesian Palau, a President was assassinated, then a second. Things move slowly in the Pacific, particularly when American and British interests are involved. Only now has an investigation of 'misconduct' started and it will take many more years before the truth will emerge − if it ever does. By then − by now, really − Palau's fate will have been sealed, too late for any chance of either economic or military independence.

But no societies deserve to remain static, even though we so often want them to. Old friends rightly argued with me over the value, or lack of it, of trying to hang on to the past. A poet friend disputed my Western habit of bemoaning the present and over-sentimentalizing the past. 'The best value we can put on our past', he said, 'is as promotion for the tourist industry.' Did the tourist industry deserve a past that rich? 'It was never that rich,' he said. Perhaps he was right. Drifting down the Karawari River on a hot afternoon, past waterside villages and passing canoes of couples fishing and collecting waterlilies, an American woman tourist suddenly complained, 'Each village is the same. There's nothing different. We've been on this river for hours, and nothing's changed.'

'But that's exactly how it is,' I found myself saying. 'That's how it is for them. Don't you see?'

A local villager travelling with us said, 'That's why I love to come home. Everything is the same as when I was a child − the river, the fishing, my family. I love coming back to my village. It's like coming back to a sort of paradise.'

'I think I'll keep on looking for mine,' someone else said.

'I think I'll do the same,' I said. 'I've only just started.'

Chapter 1

PAPUA NEW GUINEA

AT THE END OF THE RAINBOW

Papua New Guinea sits like some exotic bird of paradise to the north of Australia. Along its southern coast the seas are blue and the sunshine brilliant. At the end of day, the tropical sunset stretches across the ocean in colours that reflect the colours of the trees – flamboyant pinks, purples and reds. Inland, over the great mountain chains and the wide chocolate-covered rivers, roll vast thunder-clouds, and the rains drop vertically from the skies. At dawn, in the Highlands of Papua New Guinea, you gaze down from high above the trees into valleys partially obscured by clouds. But I never felt totally at home high in these mountains; more a coastal person, I have always preferred the scent of frangipani and the sound of the surf crashing against the reef, peaceful crystalline lagoons and languorous palm trees, to the crisp cold starry nights and damp wood-smoke of the Highland villages.

To the south-east of Papua New Guinea lies Milne Bay, the tip of the island and chains of turquoise islands. It is here that the Pacific truly begins, if you are travelling east that is, across the Solomon or Coral Seas towards the better-known islands of the South Pacific: Fiji, Tonga, Vanuatu.

Stretching east are more than six hundred islands, although most of them aren't islands at all but islets and atolls or coral reefs. Some names are familiar: the D'Entrecasteaux Islands, the Conflict Group, the Louisiade Archipelago. Best known are the Trobriands, mostly due to the work of the German anthropologist Bronislaw Malinowski, who made a lifetime's study of the social and sexual practices of the islanders. It is said that at the start of the First World War Malinowski was offered the choice of internment in Australia or banishment to the Trobriands. Wisely he chose the beautiful Trobriands, thus achieving world fame and a certain notoriety. There are hundreds more islands, of course, some without names, some without people. It was among these, at the end of the last century, that the notorious 'blackbirders' traded in human cargoes – the 'recruiting' ships kidnapping islanders to work as slave labour on the Queensland sugar estates.

When I was first there ten years ago, Milne Bay and its islands were being hard hit by drought. In Alotau, the provincial capital, a burly, hairy-chested Catholic priest wearing shorts, thongs and David-Hockney-look-alike white-framed glasses gave me coffee and home-made ginger biscuits. He suggested I meet the local government officers who were toying with the idea of developing the islands' economy by changing from the old cash crop of copra to nutmeg and black pepper. The Department of Primary Industry, the DPI, would, he said, be sending a boat out to some of the remoter islands to explore what the islanders might think about this. Might I want to hitch a lift? I might.

In the local government offices a schoolteacher was arranging to take out emergency water rations to his island, and he invited me to travel with him as far as Booker Island to see just how bad the drought was. A government boat would pick him up from Misima Island in the next few days. If I could take in my own food and water and get a plane out to Misima . . .

★

The tiny plane dropped through the clouds so low it seemed almost to skim the tops of the palm trees. Small

14

islands were scattered like random stepping-stones across the ocean. The six-seater plane was piloted by a burly Australian almost too large to fit into the pilot's seat. We bumped down on to the grass air-strip. I was met by a contact from the Fisheries Department who carried my rucksack down the dirt road that led from the air-strip to the jetty. The boat and the schoolteacher had already arrived. On the jetty the boat's Captain, small and wiry in a turquoise T-shirt and a vast sombrero, said he had no objection to taking me as far as Booker Island. From there a DPI boat would take me onwards, one of their extension officers acting as guide and interpreter.

A few yards up the grass track back towards the air-strip I found the local trade-store, a low sprawling wooden building. I appropriated a couple of large plastic containers from the owner and stocked up with tinned fish and rice. While I packed the rice into a cardboard box, he made me a rough fishing-line from an old Schweppes bottle, some nylon line and a vicious-looking hook. He tied a great lump of lead at the bottom of the line.

'Catch anything with that,' he said confidently. 'Mind you, Coca-Cola bottles are the best – the bulge makes sure your hands don't slip if you get a bite. You can even hold 'em with both hands because of their shape, but you should manage with this.'

An Englishman, he had ended up here via Australia, and a couple of broken marriages. Together we wandered back to the jetty under a mixture of frangipani and palm trees. The Captain was protesting about the amount of fresh water being loaded. He watched, furious, as it was piped into 45-gallon oil drums which were then lashed to the railings on deck. They made the ship, not particularly seaworthy in the first place, top-heavy and awkwardly bulky. There was nothing he could do, he complained: she was a government boat and he had his orders – she was to sail with as much water as she could carry. He fussed about where every drum of water should go. Realizing we would be sailing 'Papua New Guinea time', I went back to the store for a chat and a beer. Three hours later, near enough on schedule Papua New Guinea time, we lurched away from the jetty.

Chugging directly south, we made slow headway and were never out of sight of Misima's mountains until nearly sunset, which changed the ocean from a deep and startling sapphire blue to near black. When we rounded into the shallow bay off Motorina Island, where we were to berth for the night, dozens of children paddled out to meet us in mini lakatois, narrow hollowed-out canoes with a large outrigger on the side.

Two naked, giggling small boys paddled the school-teacher and me ashore and took us to see their school, a sad-looking affair of wilting palm fronds and pandanus leaves. On the walls they had pinned pictures of carrots, bananas and greens. 'Dark-green leafy vegetables = Vitamin C. Fish = Vitamin A' was written alongside in coloured pencils.

The islanders left here were mostly women – the men had left to find work in Alotau. Next to Misima's burgeoning frangipani and flame-trees, the island looked sadly derelict. There was a parched, empty feel to the place, even with the children around. Coco palms straggled alor., the grey sandy beach. The slopes were bare of gardens, the huts decrepit.

Around the edges of the lagoon the ship's crew were collecting wood and coconut husks. They left two barrels of fresh water with the women in exchange for this firewood.

The kids paddled us back to the ship. The sun dropped suddenly behind the horizon, and it was almost dark as they paddled back to their huts. Meanwhile, on deck there was a sudden roar as the coconut husks caught in the pot-bellied iron stove and orange flames belched out around our toes.

The Captain had abandoned his sombrero and was deep in an incoherent conversation with a local priest, who was travelling out to a mission hospital. It suddenly dawned on me that the Captain was not in full control of his words or movements. He was blind drunk and getting more so by the minute. The ship was being effectively run by the First Mate, while the priest and the Captain drank deeply and talked long. The Mate arranged for me to obtain my supper by fishing for it, alongside the crew. There were a few tugs at the line, but Dave's bottle and line didn't prove successful and I ended up sharing my rice with the crew in return for part of their catch.

The only other passengers, two nurses, also fishing for their supper, were unlucky as well. They were travelling to the same mission hospital as the priest, they said, and, after eating, they started to arrange their belongings on the upper deck. I couldn't understand why, when there were four small cabins below, and anyway it was beginning to rain. I picked a cabin and lumped my rucksack on to the top bunk. There was a slight, almost imperceptible movement, not much. Then the mattress moved a little more. Gingerly I lifted one corner, and armies of cockroaches shot across the cabin, up the walls, down into the lower bunk and under the mattresses again. I remembered the words of my friend, the laconic trade-store owner, standing on the jetty, beer in hand, surveying the government boat. 'The only reason that old tub keeps afloat', he said humourlessly, 'is because the cockroaches aboard are still friendly enough to hold hands.'

I heaved my rusksack down again and went outside to join the others on deck. By now the crew were there too, and it was hard to find room. I lay down between the Mate and someone else, but it was hard to sleep. The Captain was now shouting and incoherent. The priest had given up and was stretched out on deck. In his vest and underpants, the Captain clambered between us and over us, chattering in an unknown, local language. Patiently the Mate got up, took him below and put him to bed with a black coffee. From where I lay, leaning on my elbows I could see straight down the gangway into the Captain's small cabin. He would lie mumbling for a few minutes then scramble from his bunk again, demanding another beer. He would stagger up the companionway on to the deck, where, for a while, the priest took over and kept him company for an hour or two. Then he too became bored and exhausted and lay down to sleep again.

In the early hours the fine drizzle turned into a miserable wind and a hefty downpour. Cockroaches or not, everyone grabbed their sheets and vanished down to the shelter of the cabins. The Captain lay quiet for the first time that night.

By the time I woke, the sun was high. In the tropics the sun rises and is immediately overhead. Everyone had been up for hours, and we were already hugging the reef looking for the channel that would take us through to the lagoon. Booker Island looked parched and forlorn, with no trees on its low, dusty slopes. The only green came from coconut palms, which gave way halfway along the shore to mangroves. But it still had a magic, as all islands do from across the reef. On deck the Captain was transformed. In total command of his ship, he was a different man to the night before. Downing mug after mug of black coffee, he skittered about shouting instructions to the Mate, who was in the wheelhouse.

With the sun facing or directly overhead and a glassy calm sea, it's hard to find the opening in a reef. The best place to look for it is from the masthead, and that's where the Captain was for most of the time. When he wasn't hanging over the bow he hung from the mast, shouting instructions and gesticulating wildly. The schoolteacher explained that the gap in the reef was so narrow that the only way to take it was at a sharp right angle. As he spoke there was a wild waving of the Captain's right arm and we swung suddenly to starboard. The old boat juddered under the strain – we had turned almost in our own length, with barely a yard on each side of us. Shoals of fish raced for the shelter of the reef, then we were into the calm waters of the lagoon. It was still only seven o'clock.

In no other part of the world are there so many different

kinds of coral reefs, all rising from great depths and all equally dangerous: atolls, barrier reefs, atollons and shoals, or sandbanks. Discoloured water, caused by plankton or even floating volcanic matter, can give the impression of an underwater danger when none exists. Flying fish and fish spouting into the air have been mistaken for breakers and, thereby, a possible break in the reef.

The water in the lagoon was incandescent green. On shore, thatched huts fringed the bay under the shelter of the palms. From here it seemed a tropical paradise. Children played at the edge of the water. Enjoying the morning sun and calm, I took a mug of tea and joined the Mate at the stern of the ship.

'Big piss,' he said, indicating. This was the usual Papua New Guinean habit of transposing Fs and Ps. Three large fish played happily in the garbage someone was throwing over the side. Elegant, graceful things, they had broad flat heads and slender, tapering tails and were built for speed.

'Sarks,' he said pointing, 'Mummy sark and two pikinini.' I drank my tea and hoped they would eat their fill and swim away before it was time to go ashore.

Half an hour later the ship's crew rolled the barrels of fresh water over the side, straight to the bottom of the lagoon. Children paddled out to the ship in lakatois, then dived and rolled the barrels across the floor of the lagoon to shore while I waited nervously for the family of sharks to reappear. Then two cheerful small boys helped me into their canoe and paddled me ashore. Slowly, in ones and twos, the islanders were drifting to the beach. Some of them carried a kettle or a small jug or a saucepan, others just a mug – enough for their needs. The drought was eight months old, during which time they had been using sea water or brackish well water for washing and cooking, yet there was no sense of urgency in their movements. Maybe after eight months of being ignored their sense of urgency too had dried up.

The schoolteacher directed the older children to show

me to an empty hut at the end of the village that was kept for visitors. A single square hut, it was raised off the ground and made of tightly woven pandanus leaves. Pigs rustled around cheerfully underneath the steps that led up to the open doorway. It had a sparkling newness to it.

Walking along a dirt path just out of the village, an old man took me to see their gardens. It was hard to see where the path ended and the gardens began. A few sticks of kassava grew out of the dusty soil, limp and unnutritious. The old man dug in the dirt to show me the stunted growths of the kassava tubers. The soil was thin and lifeless, drifting through his fingers like fine wood-ash. He remembered better times, he said: times when the islanders had been able to grow sufficient for their needs and the needs of their children. Now the weather patterns were changing. The rains that used to arrive regularly and eased the soil for planting always arrived late. When the winds arrived they were too fierce and took away the topsoil. Their arrival was unpredictable, whereas once you had known to the hour when they would be here.

The time before the rains is known as the 'time hungry'. Now, he said, it is all time hungry. The island's economy had become one of barter. Villagers travelled as far as the neighbouring island of Pana Wina to exchange woven mats and pots for vegetables. But sometimes the sea was too high to take the canoes out.

Once upon a time these islands had traded in copra – dried coconut, used for soap manufacture – but the world no longer has need of copra. Even when it had, the prices were low. There was the added difficulty of shipping it and keeping it dry in the open canoes, particularly in high seas. Then there was the cost of storage in Alotau until it was shipped out again. As for the talk of starting an alternative cash crop – nutmeg or peppercorn – the villagers knew nothing of them, how to grow them, or whether they would grow at all on these dry, dusty slopes.

There was no quality of life here, only abject poverty. The people were thin and malnourished. The women wore what is romantically and euphemistically termed a grass skirt – in reality a covering of palm or pandanus leaves. There was an appallingly high incidence of eye disease – xeropthalmia and glaucoma – caused by vitamin-A deficiency. Yet the reefs teemed with fish, a plentiful source of vitamin A. But most of Papua New Guinea's fishing rights had been sold years earlier to the Japanese, who hoovered the reefs with lines as much as fifteen miles long, reaping the benefits. Because of the lack of iron there is an abnormally high rate of maternal deaths in these islands. Maternal death usually occurs during a woman's first pregnancy and birth. Due to insufficient iron, she is unable to expel the placenta after childbirth and slowly bleeds to death.

There was a small and well-equipped hospital ship which attempted to visit the larger islands every six weeks or so, but fickle weather or the delayed delivery of some crucial engine part could make it impossible for the floating practice ever to finish its rounds. The romance and beauty of these islands is from a distance; on shore, a terrible bleakness takes over.

It takes four years for a nutmeg tree to produce its first crop. It seemed too long for these people to wait.

That night the villagers called a meeting. A large wicker chair was found and carried into place, and someone hung a Tilly lamp from the branches of a tree. Ceremoniously they showed me to the chair.

'First of all,' said the Headman, 'we would like to thank you for bringing the water, which we needed. For this we want to thank you.'

He then asked if it could be pointed out that, welcome as the water was, it really wasn't enough. How were they to cope with the low prices of copra, the changing weather patterns, the scarce visits of the hospital ship . . .? An old man stood up at the back. He too thanked me for the fresh water, then asked if, upon my return, I could make sure that the Provincial Government knew that the last lot of water they received had been in the same type of oil drums but someone had failed to rinse them out first and the water had been undrinkable.

How was I to explain that I didn't represent Government, couldn't necessarily effect change, wouldn't necessarily even be listened to? Even so, as a whiteskin the officials would surely have to take notice of me. They had been ignored too long these patient, polite people.

The next day I toured the island properly, but no corner of it seemed to offer hope for growing anything.

The government ship with its drunken Captain took off with the remainder of the water, the priest and the two nurses towards Sudest, and I waited for the DPI boat to arrive. Arrive she did, and for once right on time. This little boat made the government ship look like an ocean liner. Little more than a dinghy, she bobbed cheerfully in the lagoon with a dog-eared canopy flapping desultorily over the engine casing. We were to leave, said Simon, the rural extension officer, before dawn, at 4.30. There had been engine problems, and they needed to get the boat back to Bwagaoia, on Misima, before continuing. I was ashamed at my sense of relief at leaving the miserable island.

We left in the morning blackness as the village slept, one of the villagers sleepily paddling us across the lagoon to the little boat. It was still dark as we chugged alongside the shore, following the path I had taken with the old man, past the mangroves. The crew of four drank sweet tea and polished the engine, singing cheerfully and cracking jokes among themselves. We were outside the reef as the first light of dawn broke, and excitedly they got out the lines and started to trawl for fish. Dolphins played alongside, and flying fish took off and skimmed across our decks while the crew pulled in barracuda, king-fish and Spanish mackerel and strung them along the narrow deck. Then, somewhere in the middle of the Coral Sea, the engine gave a cough, spluttered and died. Until now I hadn't thought of the size or seaworthiness of the little boat. Now we sat, motionless, in the middle of a sea that ran at us sideways on. The beam sea caused the boat to corkscrew and bob, rise and sink. The waves were huge. We sank into a well between waves and then rose again to the top of the next one.

As the sun rose higher in the sky, the temperature soared. The crew worked on the engine, singing cheerfully. They took it to pieces and put it back together again. When that didn't work, they repeated the process. Neither sea nor heat affected them; they sang as they worked. Simon abandoned his agricultural training and dug deep into the engine with them. Eight hours later there was a tiny splutter from beneath the canopy and a cheer from the crew. They started the engine and headed for home.

The waves were very high now, and each time we surfaced one the crew had to cut the engine. We zig-zagged madly towards the horizon, taking each wave three-quarters on, heading up it and throttling back as we got to the top. The engine was sounding feebler and feebler, but held out. I sat at the prow, fingers crossed. I could see Misima on the horizon, then an hour later, as the light was going, it was close enough to swim to. We hugged the shore until we reached the jetty. A small, cheerful crowd awaited us. Excited children hurled themselves into the brown water. They had spotted our slow and unsure approach hours ago. Dave, the trade-store owner, was among them.

'We were going to give you another couple of days before we alerted Alotau,' he said cheerily. 'That old tub's always getting into trouble. 'Course, even if we'd been able to get through to them on the radio, there's no guarantee they'd have been able to get a plane for a few days.'

It took two days for the earth to stop rocking and rolling beneath my feet. A British volunteer working for the Fisheries Department gave me a bed, and I waited for the tiny four-seater plane out to Alotau. The day it arrived another boat was berthed at the jetty. The plane got a flat tyre, and Dave talked me into taking the boat back instead. I didn't need much persuasion. Two more days between the islands was irresistible. We were due to leave the next morning but, true to Pacific time-keeping, didn't steam off until afternoon. The ship was full of ladies and babies, and we eased away from the Bwagaoia jetty into a sea like glass with a soft mist rising from its surface. The little boat ran a sort of bus-stop route along Misima's shore. Village bells rang out as the boat was spotted, and canoes came alongside from the villages hidden in bays and creeks and mangrove swamps. Women and children were loaded into the canoes and paddled cheerily home, their gossip ringing across a sea flat as a lake. The haze lifted late in the afternoon, allowing the beginnings of a picturebook Pacific sunset. There were golden apricot clouds, and shafts of pink light hit the dark sea, colouring it purple.

We pulled into a small bay to berth for the night. Small boys paddled their canoes out to meet us. They paddled me ashore on to a silver beach and took me by the hand through a winding path at the base of a cliff. High above was rain-forest. A waterfall crashed on to the river bed, its heart high somewhere in the rain-forest. Someone had thoughtfully erected a bent piece of corrugated iron where the waterfall cascaded finally into the river. I dodged round behind it and showered in the fresh, ice-cold water. The children politely turned their back and wandered off to gossip among themselves until I re-emerged clean and changed, then they led me back down the track and paddled me back to the ship as dusk was falling.

On deck the Captain had put up a small washing-line and was hanging out T-shirts and shorts and lap-laps. On shore the villagers, their way lit by flaming torches of palm and pandanus, were exchanging firewood for coconuts and fish with the ship's crew. The sea had turned from purple to black. The waterfall shone high above – a silver ribbon cutting through the black-green of the rain-forest. It was a magical scene. I turned to the Captain wondering how I could express my admiration but he was busy fiddling with a transistor radio, putting in new batteries.

As he slotted in a very worn and obviously favourite cassette, there faded up through the stillness a mournful refrain. Across the bay warbled Engelbert Humperdinck's plea to let him go, release him, make him free. The Captain grinned at me cheerfully and gave me the thumbs up.

★

It was seven years since I had made that trip, and its spell had stayed with me more than that of any other trip I had made in Papua New Guinea. Now I had come back. In Port Moresby's Jackson's Airport, a liver and white sniffer dog cheerfully examined the baggage on the carousel. Both the carousel and the dog were new, and burly Australians in sharply pressed shorts and knee-socks queued patiently, carrying briefcases and metal boxes with Placer and Broken Hill stickers on them. The new Pacific cowboys – prospectors and mining men.

Flying up from Australia I had sat next to a genial Aussie from Western Australia – mining country. 'You can be sure when the economic miracle happens Papua New Guinea isn't going to see any of it,' he said. 'The people will emigrate to where the mines are. It'll depress the copra industry. The country will have to start importing food. The mining companies are the ones who'll make the profit, you can be sure. The locals will be the last people to see any of it.'

Yet these changes were already under way. There had been no real copra trade when I had visited the islands seven years earlier, and Papua New Guinea had been importing its fish, tinned, from Japan for years. He was, however, the second person that week to talk about Papua New Guinea's forthcoming economic miracle.

On a hot Saturday afternoon in Sydney's western suburbs I had sat watching while an old friend struggled to put up a garden fence. He had a reputation for being something of an economic whizz-kid and had worked for several years in Papua New Guinea's National Planning

Office as an economic adviser. During his time there, he had moved in the elevated circles of government planners, World Bank officials and visiting economic advisers. In those days I had been somewhat in awe of him.

'Do you know, in six or seven years PNG will be sitting on mineral resources worth $300 million a year?' Harry said. 'That's the same as it receives in untied aid from Australia. PNG is a gold mine waiting to be tapped. Oil too. Hang on to this a moment would you?' he asked, sweating over a support post.

'So how do they manage the boom? Everybody knows in theory how you handle a recession, but how do you handle a boom?' – Harry leaned across the fence and looked at me pointedly. 'You don't usually have to deal with that kind of problem,' he said.

He was right. Over a three-year period, Papua New Guinea had discovered more gold than any other country in the world. One mine, on Lihir, an island off the coast of New Ireland, is potentially the largest in the world – larger than anything in South Africa or Russia. Alongside the gold there are cobalt and nickel, chrome and timber, several billion cubic feet of gas and, if the oil strikes are successful, billions of barrels of that too. As big as anything in Saudi Arabia. Unlike other Pacific islands, scraping along on coconut economies, Papua New Guinea offers what the economists describe as 'prospects of real and sustained economic growth'. This is not anything new for Papua New Guinea, but it does present a whole load of problems that are markedly different to those of the first great gold rush sixty years ago.

When I had first accepted a job in Papua New Guinea in 1979, there was a variety of confusions as to where it was, Ghana being the most common. Guinea-Bissau, Guyana and French Guinea were second guesses. Finally there would be recall of the large, humpbacked, dragon-shaped island at the top of Australia, the southern part of which, Papua, had once been pink.

The aid agency I was to work for showed us a series of

documentary films as part of our training. Mostly they featured strange anthropological rites in which nearly naked people wearing a brief covering of paint and leaves took part in things called sing-sings and mumus and pig-kills. It had little to do with the Papua New Guinea of the twenty-first century, and when I finally flew in from Hong Kong I was surprised to do so in a jet.

Arriving at the capital, Port Moresby, at dawn it hadn't looked like my idea of a tropical island. There were no great rain-forests, mountain ranges or rushing rivers to be seen from the plane window. This was coastal savannah country, dry and dusty. The earth and surrounding low hills had a burnt, scorched look. The mountains and rain-forests were to come later.

Now it looked exactly the same as it had then, browner if anything. The plane was two-thirds empty, those on board mostly returning Australian contract workers. We waited patiently while a red carpet and a brass band were rolled out in honour of the Governor-General, who was also on the flight, before stepping out into stupefying heat. That was something I had forgotten. Papua New Guinea has two climates: hot and wet or hot and dry. Moresby is hot and usually dry. The heat bounced off the hills, rolled along the tarmac and sizzled up the backs of my legs, turning them bright red in seconds. We hurried towards the covered passageway and positioned ourselves under the overhead fans in the terminal building.

People today still talk of Papua New Guinea as 'the last unknown', the title of Gavin Souter's superb, but now dated, book, and refer to its inhabitants as 'stone-age'. There is some truth in the clichés, but only some. Tribal wars still take place with startling regularity over land, pigs or women. Driving through the Highlands once, I came across a cheerful group of men and children in the freezing early-morning drizzle, their bodies painted in fierce yellow and carrying spears and bows and arrows. In recent times PNG has proved a wonderful working laboratory for all kinds of development theoreticians.

I remember an aid worker telling me why: 'you can see things getting done here,' she said. 'That's its advantage over Africa.'

The country's first contacts with Europeans were brief and often bloody, and have to a certain extent remained that way. It was probably a Portuguese, Jorge de Meneses, who, in 1526, was the first white man to set foot on the island. He was categoric in his denunciation of the island, proclaiming that the devil walked with the people.

During the second half of the nineteenth century the islands saw their own devils: the first blackbirders 'recruiting' labour for the Queensland sugar estates; the whalers, traders, prospectors and missionaries. Alan Moorehead first used the phrase 'fatal impact' of Tahiti and the French Polynesian islands, but Papua New Guinea has suffered as many fatal impacts as the rest of the Pacific – perhaps more: colonization by the Germans in the north, the arrival of The Australian Squadron to claim the southern half for Queen Victoria, the Japanese occupation, followed by Australian administration.

Holland, of course, made its own impact – a lasting one – by simply proclaiming the western half of the island to be Dutch. For almost a hundred years the Australians and the Dutch had shared their common border. Things went smoothly enough until the Second World War, at the end of which was an all-out colonial war between the Dutch and the Indonesian nationalists. The argument carried on through the fifties and into the early sixties when the then Indonesian President, Sukarno, flexing his muscles, started a massive arms build-up with the intention of 'liberating' New Guinea. In 1962 the two sides finally got together under the auspices of the United Nations, and Dutch New Guinea was transferred to Indonesia. There had been neither representation nor involvement on behalf of the West Papuans during the negotiations.[1] Overnight, one million people were yanked out of a Melanesian culture and into an Indonesian/Muslim one. That conflict persists today, Indonesia's transmigration policy systematically shifting vast numbers of people from the overcrowded islands of Java and Bali on to what is now called Irian Jaya, while the West Papuans are forced further and further into the interior or flee across the border. There are something in the region of ten thousand refugees from Western Papua – Irian Jaya – in refugee camps along the Papua New Guinea border, a fact almost unknown, and certainly unaddressed, in the West.

Geographically the country is extraordinary. Great mountain ranges cut horizontally through the centre of the island. There are deep fjords on the northern coast, malarial swamps in the south-west; the Chambri Lakes of the Sepik region and mile-wide yellow rivers cutting through dripping wet, malaria-infested rain-forest in the Purari Delta. There are savannah in the south and chains of islands to the east. It is a country of over one thousand tribes and more than seven hundred languages – not dialects, but languages.

In the Highlands, coffee has made many a highlander a 'big man', and a highlander will think nothing of buying a Toyota Land Cruiser outright in cash made from the profits of coffee. Yet in a village in the south-west, on the side of the Purari River, I have seen a woman batten herself in from the spirits and ghosts that she swore to me were out and about that night.

Back in Port Moresby, outside Jackson's Airport, a sign on the wall forbade the chewing and spitting of betel-nut. It was stained scarlet from having been spat at. A tall welcome-palm shaped like an open fan stood on a patch of yellowed grass, its fronds curling and brown at the edges. It had stood there for decades, long before there had even been an airport. It was the end of October and hot as hell. Driving the short distance into the town, the hills were brown and dusty with a scattering of stunted ghost gums. Not a blade of grass anywhere.

The problem with Moresby is that it has no centre and no heart. It is an ugly, sprawling series of unlovely suburbs scattered between and over sunbaked hills. Its architecture, often described as Australian tropical, is Queensland-style houses, raised off the ground and with fly-wiring over the windows. The residential areas are interrupted by small-scale, concrete-and-glass shopping plazas. Only part of the existing old town of Port Moresby still has some charm about it, a kind of Pacific-colonial.

The lack of thought and planning given to Moresby is reflected in the names of its suburbs: Two-Mile, Four-Mile, Six-Mile, Three-Mile Hill. Occasionally a more exotic name will creep in – Korobosea, Waigani, Hohola. But there's never been anything exotic about living in these suburbs. Stories of Port Moresby's rascal gangs are legion, and houses too easily broken into with bush knives are made as impenetrable as possible by security fencing, lights, watchdogs and electronic alarms, giving some of the larger houses a South American feel.

Moresby has experienced the fate of all Third World capital cities: urban drift. Migrants from the depressed rural areas, together with school drop-outs looking for opportunities to better their lives, have arrived by boat from the coastal areas, by plane from the Highlands. They converge on relatives and fellow-villagers who, under Papua New Guinean traditional laws of reciprocity, are duty-bound to give them bed, board and food. So the urban areas have divided into clans, and the pressures on land, housing and jobs have grown in parallel with inter-clan rivalry and fighting.

However unlovely its architecture, I had been enchanted by my first experience of actually living in the tropics. My ugly house was surrounded by a hibiscus hedge, and in the mornings men and women walking by on their way to work used to stop and select a flower which they would tuck into their hair or behind an ear. At sunset, the family who lived in the boy-house at the end of the garden – a remnant from the colonial era – would sit out and cook over an open fire in the garden. I hadn't been there long when Koko gave birth to a daughter. Her husband, Lahvi, knocked at my door.

'Excuse me, missus,' he said politely, 'I'd like to have a farty.'

Slightly taken aback, I then remembered that Papua New Guineans have problems with Fs and Ps, transposing them.

It wouldn't be a problem, I assured him.

Extra politely, he said he was planning to have an 'extra big farty in a couple of weeks' time'.

No problem, I said.

A few days later a truck called, laden with branches of trees which were piled up against the sides of the boy-house. Then another arrived carrying sacks of rice. About a week after that the first guests arrived, coastal people from Lahvi's village. They cheerfully moved in and started digging a vast pit in the garden, a respectful distance from my house. This was the oven, or mumu. Stones would be heated over a fire; the food, in its coconut cream, would be wrapped in banana leaves and buried (although many Papua New Guineans opt for tinfoil as well); the hot stones would be put on top, as would the earth, and the lot would be left to bake for hours in the sun. The group around the evening fire expanded. More and more trucks arrived, bringing food that would be cheaper to buy in the village than here in Moresby – great arms of bananas and taro leaves. One day I drove straight past my house, not recognizing the groups of women and children sitting in the drive sheltering from the sun under black umbrellas.

Finally the Sunday of the farty arrived, and lorry-load after lorry-load of cheerful coastal families appeared. At about two they came over to the house and invited me to the mumu. The women dragged away the palm leaves and hot stones from the pit, while Koko showed off her baby, Julie, and we sat round cross-legged on woven mats and tucked into roast pig and chicken and taro and sweet potato, cooked in coconut cream. The celebrations continued until well after nightfall – cheerful, but low key. But then Koko and Lahvi, and probably the whole of their village too, were Seventh Day Adventists, and so no beer

31

was present. At dawn, the first trucks, cars and vans started to rumble away, and a few days later everything was in order again – but I think I had preferred it before.

A few months later a state of emergency – sadly, the first of several – was declared in Port Moresby with the idea of making sure that the rascal gangs returned to their squatter settlements at night. In a show of bravado, or maybe something more menacing, one rascal-gang leader announced to the local politicians, 'We determine Papua New Guinea's image abroad; we control the country's economy; we are the carpet you walk on; and we are your time bombs.'

One of the results of this eloquent declaration of warfare has been to change the shape of Moresby's skyline. The brown hills above the curve of Moresby's Ela Beach are now bursting with a very non-tropical form of real estate: high-rise, concrete-block apartments that offer rascal-proof security to those who can afford it.

The phenomenon of the gangs is proving fertile ground for social anthropologists, but it has proved an area of worry for the politicians. How do you enforce law and order in a society with its roots deep in payback killings and tribal warfare? Crime against the state is a very abstract concept within Papua New Guinean society, it can't always be accountable. There are spirits and other reasons. In any local court you will see puri-puri – magic – blamed for people's irrational or anti-social behaviour. These things make the procedures of law and order very unworkable. Police and patrol officers are fearful of going into areas from which they do not come. The rascals themselves are aware and confident of their power. But the violence is not confined to youth: there are plenty of adult men with jobs and social-standing who contribute as much to the violence of the society as unemployed youths.

Over dinner one night, I heard the story of how the Premier of one of the provinces was out drinking at the local small inn overlooking the ocean. Nobody knew what triggered it, but suddenly he went on the rampage, assault-

The government boat moored off Booker Island, after delivering emergency water supplies. (Milne Bay District, Papua New Guinea)

Korevake village in the Purari Delta, Papua New Guinea.

Urun, Ricky and Cinderella playing houses. (Madang, Papua New Guinea)

A meeting house in the Sepik region – the heartland of Papua New Guinean art and culture.

A sacred kassowary bird stands in front of a Sepik spirit house.

A baby asleep in a bilum, the Papua New Guinean string bag, which is the country's unofficial emblem.

ing the cook, the manager and the manager's wife, who were Europeans. In a drunken rage he told them to get out of the country. He wanted all whites out of the country. Someone called the police, but he sent them away. They went, of course! When the *Post Courier* newspaper rang the Provincial Government to check the story, they were told that the Premier had been assaulted in the restaurant.

'I have few illusions left any more,' a friend who had witnessed the event said. 'This town is run by gangsters on a senseless power-trip, wanting bunce, kick-backs, anything that's going as a consolidation and manifestation of their power. Cargo cult is still very much alive here.'

Cargo cults started to spring up in Melanesia after the first contact with European traders and missionaries. They were an attempt to both explain and acquire the wealth that was so obviously in the hands of the whites. In a subsistence economy with no notion of profit, investments or savings, Papua New Guineans believed that only the Europeans had access to the goods they coveted, and if not to the goods themselves, certainly to the ways and means of obtaining them. They thought that if their own leaders could re-create the rituals and sorcery through which the whites must obtain cargo then they too would come by the goods. Inextricably and confusedly caught up between their old beliefs and the new religions many Melanesians believed that the goods would also bring spiritual salvation.

Many anthropologists have sought to explain cargo cults as a precursor to nationalism, the first form of popular rebellion and a bid for independence from European rule and economic domination.

My friend, however, was cynical about that being the motivation today.

'Now it's not so much a cult as cargoism. Remember that 'ism, it's very important. What you have here today is rampant neo-colonialism and all the classic things are starting to happen,' he said dispiritedly.

★

I flew north to see friends in Madang on the north coast. Once you leave Port Moresby, the magic of Papua New Guinea becomes clearer as you fly over the densely forested Owen Stanley Range. We curled over the Huon Peninsula and flew alongside the coast, this time by the Finisterre Range, rugged and unfriendly. Flying in Papua New Guinea is beautiful and scaring. The weather closes in suddenly; massive clouds build up and obscure mountain passes too quickly for comfort. And the mountains form the central backbone of the island – twelve, thirteen and fourteen thousand feet high.

Madang is a pretty, sleepy little tropical town. Its half-dozen dusty streets are rich in shade trees: jacaranda, frangipani, flame-trees and, my favourites, African tulip-trees. The town sits on the point of a peninsula jutting out between Astrolabe Bay and the Bismarck Sea, and a chain of islands stretches from the harbour north along the coast.

When the Germans arrived here towards the end of the last century, the north coast was infested with malarial swamps. They drained off the brackish water, replacing it with sea water and creating a series of ponds and waterways which helped sustain a feeling of coolness and tranquillity amidst the humidity. Germany's Neu Guinea Kompanie was ruthless in acquiring land, exploiting the locals and keeping the missions out. New Guinea was theirs, and the last thing they needed was any missionary activity. 'We don't like to have the missions or missionaries nearby because they are our conscience and therefore undesirable and inconvenient,' they stated flatly. In the end the missions won, but not entirely. They had as little idea of local culture and customs as the Administration, and they stood by passively as it went about its business. The locals saw them as part of the Administration, and in sixteen years they didn't make a single convert.

Thirteen years before the Germans there came an extraordinary Russian scientist, Baron Niklai Miklouho Maclay. He recorded language and culture and explored the

Finisterre foothills. He called the coast by his own name and where he landed Constantine Harbour, after his patron Grand Duke Constantine, the President of the Imperial Russian Geographical Society.

Maclay arrived with a Polynesian servant and a Swedish sailor. The Polynesian died, and the Swede, according to Maclay's diaries, was constantly ill and a perpetual nuisance. Some thought Maclay to be the spirit of a departed ancestor, and certainly others thought he was from the moon and used to ask him about life there. Maclay was seen as a source of wealth (gifts) and super-human knowledge.

When the Polynesian died, Maclay buried him secretly at sea and, when asked where he had gone, pointed vaguely and mysteriously at the horizon. 'It was assumed the man had flown away . . .'

When Dr Otto Finsch, representing the Neu Guinea Kompanie, took possession of the north-east mainland and the Bismarck Archipelago in 1884, Maclay was appalled, telegraphing Bismarck and Tsar Alexander to point out the injustice of the German's step and the reluctance of the locals to be annexed. Although sympathetic, the Russians did not at that time want to enter into a dispute with Germany. The British, whom he had also approached, found it easier to come to an agreement with Germany over carving up the Pacific. And so the entire archipelago, including New Britain and New Ireland, the North Solomons, Bougainville, Choiseul and Isabel, were to become part of Germany's empire, as was Western Samoa. The British informed Maclay that in future when it came to matters concerning the Maclay Coast he would be consulting only with the Germans.

Maclay returned to Russia in 1886 and died two years later, aged forty-two. Tragically, through a misunderstanding and because she did not speak Russian, his English wife subsequently burned almost everything he had ever written, and so his life and malaria-torn months in New Guinea still remain something of a mystery.

It was black night when the plane landed at Madang, sticky and humid – far hotter than Moresby had been. On the flight up from Moresby, a small, mousy woman had sat next to me.

'Do you know where you are going?' she asked a short while after take off.

'Oh yes. I've been to Madang before.'

She smiled. 'I didn't mean that.' As she handed me several tracts, I realized that she referred to greater travels than those inside Papua New Guinea. She said she represented the New Tribes Mission.

'Our work here is to translate the word of Our Lord into their Tok Ples,' she said. Tok Ples is the local language. The natives, the missionary told me, had recently made their desires known to New Tribes: they wanted to read the scriptures in their own local languages, not the more commonly used pidgin. This, she said, was the current thrust of New Tribes' work in Papua New Guinea. 'Today, in West New Britain alone,' she explained, 'the mission have three planes and one helicopter to take the word of the Lord, translated of course, into the remoter areas.'

In addition to the planes and helicopter, she said, two air-strips had been built.

I was surprised they had those kinds of resources. Although many of the missions had planes, and I was used to seeing priests as pilots ferrying food and supplies in and out from the remoter mission stations, I'd thought of them as a necessary means of transport rather than an asset to evangelizing.

'We aren't paid,' the mousy woman said, 'but Christians in New Zealand who work, contribute. He provides for our needs – not our wants, but for our needs.' The mission's headquarters, she added, was in the United States.

I ventured that the majority of Papua New Guineans had their own beliefs and should, perhaps, be left to them. She looked shocked.

'The people here believe in spirits, and they live in fear of them. Animism is a terrible belief, based only on fear. We offer them a choice. The choice is eternal salvation.'

'Or?'

'Eternal damnation or eternal salvation.'

I said I felt that this did not present a whole host of options.

'If they see the fear of what's coming and it shows them the way to God, which is the right way, that's fine,' the woman said fervently. 'Anything that brings them to the Lord is the right way.'

Spitefully I told her of a Papua New Guinean friend who, as a child, had been brought up on a mission. One evening we were sitting under a frangipani tree, warding off mosquitoes. 'Before I was born,' Olivia had said, 'my parents were sure I was going to be a boy. Then, as I grew up, they expected of me all the things they would have had I been a boy. They wanted me to be a teacher, so when I was ten they sent me away to the Anglican Mission to be educated. There was this lady teacher from Australia and me and three other kids. I just remember Sunday mornings and making that brown stuff. What do you call it? Gravy. Every Sunday making gravy. Stirring it with a spoon. That's what I remember from mission education.'

The woman from New Tribes was unimpressed and left me some tracts to read.

At Madang airport the woman from New Tribes was met by a group of Papua New Guineans wearing T-shirts proclaiming they were 'ol sip sip bilong Jesus' – Jesus' flock. One other T-shirt stood out at the airport: a clenched fist holding up an AK47 in salute. 'Coup Fiji 1987,' it read – 'I've been there.'

★

The headlights of the Land Cruiser picked out frangipani and banana palms. The town looked luscious and green. That night, over dinner among old friends, I heard for the first time new words in the Papua New Guinea lexicon:

corruption, bribes, insider dealing.

'It sounds,' I said, 'like Nigeria.'

'That's right,' said a jaded friend. 'The future is definitely along African lines. There are 106 individuals in Parliament aligning themselves to their own interests.'

The news that Papua New Guinea's former Defence Minister, Ted Diro, had accepted bribes from the commander of the Indonesian armed forces was reverberating around the dinner table. There were rumours that it was all part of a plan for Indonesia to dominate the entire Pacific region. The two countries had shared a troubled border for years. With the continuing breakdown of law and order, uncontrolled tribal fighting in Enga, and forty ministers, including a former Prime Minister, facing misconduct charges, there were many, including army officers, who were deeply unhappy at the state of the country. The Fijian coup had made a big impression in PNG. Despite the Prime Minister's denials, it could be that the widespread civil unrest might tempt the army to play a more active role in the running of the country. Many Europeans were wondering just how secure the Government's hold was on the armed forces. Against this background, the Diro affair was opening up more cracks than it papered over.

The reason the news had more than usual impact was due as much to the political fragility of the then Wingti Government as to the powerful, politically hardline Mr Diro. In a statement to Parliament Mr Diro maintained that he had taken the bribes 'for the good of PNG'. He stated that the inability of the current leadership to address the problems of rising unemployment, the law and order issue and foreign control of the economy meant that everyone was sitting on a time bomb, and that all the ingredients for a coup existed, now, in Papua New Guinea.

The peaceful oasis I was hoping for seemed as unattainable in sleepy Madang as in Moresby.

'Madang is a one-cow town, with the same problems as Port Moresby,' somebody said. 'Gangs of disillusioned, anti-establishment youth are walking the streets. And white skins make you stand out. There aren't enough whiteskins to hit at, so they attack their own.'

The rains came that night, bouncing and clattering down on the tin roof, stopping almost as quickly as they had arrived.

I woke to church bells and brilliant sun. The house belonged to the Anglican mission. The rains had come and gone. Outside, the grass was covered with a cream carpet of fallen frangipani flowers. The children were calling out to each other.

'Good morning, Libby,' screamed Angus, Alison and Jay's exuberant red-haired son. 'Good morning, Erin. Good morning, Cinderella.'

The little girls called dutifully back, 'How are you Angus?'

The mission tenants were happy to see the rains. They hadn't paid their rents or their water bills or their electricity bills for some time. 'Why should they?' Alison said. 'They live outside most of the time. In effect they can have free housing. They have no need for light, and when the rains come they can use tank water.'

An old friend, Will Guthrie, was taking me to lunch and to talk. Will had been in PNG for almost twenty-three years. The former love he held for the country was waning, leaving him jaded and talking of 'going finish'. We rattled north in his old car along a compacted coral road, winding our windows up against the dust thrown up by the occasional passing bus. We passed mile after mile of coconut-palm plantations that had once been part of the Neu Guinea Kompanie's empire and were now part of the Catholic Church's. Children ran out from villages so well hidden among the trees that, until you heard the shrieks of excitement, you didn't know they existed. The sight of a car and two whiteskins still managed to excite them to a frenzy of half delight, half fear.

The plantations ended suddenly at the edge of a white sand beach. 'You know,' said Will, 'when Margaret Mead came back to address the university, she said that the thing that would save PNG was its diversity of races, tribes and languages. There were others, of course, who always held the view that the highlanders would take over the coastals when they came to Moresby. But they didn't, and they don't do it in Parliament. Perhaps they're too busy squabbling. Do you know, the Enga are the largest language group, but spend all their time fighting each other.

'You know, the police killed a rascal here, and the local people put up road-blocks against the police, even though they didn't know who the rascals were – they meant nothing to them.

'The contempt for the police has always been there. I remember being on a boat in 1969. As the boat was docking at the wharf, a local guy pointed at a policeman standing there and made some offensive remark, the point of which was that they were useless. I remember being quite shocked at the time. Now I would have to agree with him.'

More recently a white inspector had arrived from Lae. He had been about a year in the service. He was tired. 'You have to understand,' he said to Will, 'the police is just another government department, therefore it's just as inefficient as every other government department. That's the way you have to look at it.'

There is also the perennial problem of payback. Payback is the Papua New Guinean eye for an eye, but it makes any system of law and order unworkable because not only is it an eye for an eye but it is also the rule of obligation gone mad. Nobody is going to give evidence against an offender if they know that his entire clan is geared to taking up arms in defence of his honour, guilty or not. That applies to the police too, whose commitment to preserving their own and their clan's well-being exceed their commitment to any upholding of law and order.

We sat in a far-away hotel having lunch. The waves crashed on the shore. Nothing and nobody passed by on the dusty road outside. It should have been paradise.

'People are clutching at straws,' said the hotel-owner, a naturalized Papua New Guinean. 'They don't see successive Governments as having done anything for them. There has been – is – overwhelming disappointment with Governments since Independence. What you have here is not so much a multi-party or even a one-party system as a no-party system. They have control but don't know how to use it.'

'Corruption and nepotism,' said a white man at the bar. 'Even when someone is qualified to do a job, it's hard to keep them. They'll go to Moresby. Then there'll be someone to take over, but he won't have been trained.'

He was talking of his own job. He had spent year after year training Papua New Guineans to take over from him when he left. Each time it had been the same story.

'You have to understand,' said Will, 'people still harbour the idea that they can go back to the village. And, of course, they can.'

★

It was impossible to escape the preoccupation with violence. Alison, with whom I was staying, was working on a public-awareness campaign to make women, and men, realize that being beaten was not part of the marital contract. It had taken effort to persuade the police that wife-beating was as much an offence as rape. In rural areas the police too often saw little use in completing crime reports, as they were completely unable to pursue any kind of successful investigation.

Pack rape, it seems, is a peculiarly Papua New Guinean phenomenon. The headlines in the *Post Courier* made blood-chilling reading and reflected massive sexual violence against women: 'Nun Pack-Raped by Six'; 'Fishing Night Ends in Gang Rape of Wife'; 'Popondetta Woman Pack-Raped by Four Sepiks'; Woman's Tongue Cut Out in Tribal Conflict'. On the next page there was a feature on the making of a film to boost PNG's image overseas: a Danish film company was here to make a promotional film about the country called *Realities and Dreams*.

Alison showed me a report in which it said that, in Port Moresby's National Capital District, the rape figure for the first six months of 1985 had been twice as high as the highest rate reported in any American city. Workshops held by the university and the Department of Community Medicine at the general hospital during the state of emergency reported that two cases of rape or sexual assault were presented to the hospital every week, fifty per cent of them under the age of sixteen.

One night we heard on the radio that, as part of the new law-and-order campaign, a catechist and reserve police-man named Augustine was to hold a meeting a few miles down the coast at Alexishafen, the original German settlement and mission. The meeting was to take place in the market-place. Its aim was to inform women of their rights when it came to being beaten up by their husbands.

We drove through the early morning mist past the same coco-palm plantations as Will and I had passed the previous day. In the small covered market-place of Alexishafen, women and men sat cross-legged on the stone floors of the market. Augustine and the local police inspector, Kiassi, had started by reading the women their rights.

'If man bilong you breakim skin, bruise eye, brek nose, em grievous bodily harm. Em a criminal offence,' said Augustine, neat in the dark-blue shirt and shorts of the police force.

There were many more women than men. They passed betel-nut around and breast-fed their babies. 'What if I go out with another man and my husband beats me up and he goes to prison? What happens when he comes out?' asked one of the women.

'Em now,' said Kiassi, 'Adultery is a very serious issue. That's provocation. You married eye bilong God, eye bilong community, emi wrong to breakim.'

The few men present started to hijack the meeting. 'Me buy meri emi go pinis, now me got right go fight em. Man nogat onepela right?'

My pidgin was rusty; I was having a hard time keeping up with him. A girl from Alison's office whispered to me, giggling. 'He says, "If I have paid bride-price and she leaves me, then I can treat her any way I want." '

'Look,' said the inspector. 'You buy a car for ten or fifteen thousand kina. You go along the road, you crash the car and go to jail for irresponsible driving – it's a waste of money. Same with bride-price.' He beamed at the irrefutable logic of this, only to be caught out by the next question.

'What if I've got two wives,' asked one of the men. 'Can I go to prison for that?' There were shrieks of laughter as this brought it a little nearer home. Papua New Guineans always combined intense shyness with extreme forthrightness.

A cheeky, skinny girl chewing a great wodge of betel-nut asked what would happen if she was at a meeting like this and her husband turned up and pulled her out of it. Suppose he then took her home and beat her up. Would he go to prison? The question hit the spot. Augustine and Kiassi looked at each other awkwardly.

Augustine admitted that two hours hadn't been nearly enough. 'But at least people will start discussing their rights,' he said.

Driving back through town, Alison said to me, 'Look at these images of Western culture,' We were outside the Tropical Cinema. A small crowd watched the posters being changed for the weekend programmes: *Vengeance Squad*, *Ninja Exterminators*, *Remo Unarmed* and *Dangerous Dangerous* were on offer for the Saturday matinee, followed by *Death Before Dishonour* and *Legacy of Rage*. 'Can you wonder we have these problems?' Alison said, 'We're seen as glamorous, promiscuous, available.'

She was right, of course. At the tiny video shop opposite

the low, sprawling post office there were shelves of the stuff: *Armed Response*; *Fear City*. 'Out of the depths of New York's night-life', said the cover blurb, 'emerges a self-righteous, sadistic killer who is out to punish the evil elements of mankind. . . . Suspense-filled sequences . . .'

Waiting in the car outside the local Steamships – the Woolworths of the Pacific – a human-size Mickey Mouse with an oversize papier-mâché head was handing out Fanta and Coca-Cola. Inside, a sign proclaimed the week's best video value. 'Highly recommended,' it read, 'this week's videospecial: *Vasectomy, a Personal Matter*.'

That night a group of us sat on the terrace of the Smugglers Inn, drinking beer and watching the sun setting over the Bismarck Sea. The flying foxes filled the sky over the ocean, and the normally boisterous Angus sipped his orange juice thoughtfully. Shadowy figures walked along the sea-front under the great casuarina trees. It was a tropical night as tropical nights are meant to be, and a meeting of old friends. Two of them had taken out Papua New Guinean citizenship and were now wondering whether it had been a wise move.

'The country is being ruled by oafs and buffoons,' said the woman, 'and, you know, the sexual mythology of the white woman is still dominant. You get harassment and the demanding of favours. Sex on the office floor. Pornography and hang-ups in high office. And people are challenging the police all the way. And Papua New Guinean men have adapted to the Western life-style like ducks to water – the symbols of power. Despite what they say about whites, they're doing the same things – sending their children to international schools, so subsidizing the education of expatriate children who have an allowance for that anyway. Unless we get some good people in power, this country's had it.'

I was sad to hear it, but she knew better than me. She was open and outspoken, and I wondered how safe the country would remain for her.

As we drove back along the sea-front, flames lit up the

darkness. Groups of people sitting under the casuarinas had lit fires at their bases. Alison, normally the calmest person in the world, suddenly said angrily, 'Look at that. What is all this shit about natives being at one with their environment?'

★

The Purari is a great, grey-green, greasy Limpopo of a river. Grey mud clings to its banks, which are green with overhanging palms and bread-fruit. Whether it is the greyness of the mud or the greyness of the skies I'm not sure, but the nipa and sago are as vivid as the emerald green in a child's paintbox. From the air, the river and its tributaries are chocolate-brown and topaz; the bush black and mosquito-ridden. I once knew someone who had come here and contracted malaria twice in five weeks.

Korevake village stood high on the banks of the river. Like all the river villages, it was dependent on the sago palm for everything – housing, flooring, clothing and cooking utensils, but most of all for food. This is a different kind of sago to school puddings, looking and tasting like alabaster or talcum powder, dry and sticking uncomfortably to the roof of the mouth.

A nutritionist friend, Stan, was doing a long-term survey on the part played by sago in the diet of the local people. 'You can come along if you want to,' he said, 'but you'll have to work.' That suited me well. I was to stay with a family and note how they cooked their sago, how much they ate and how often.

The twin Otter made a series of bus-stop hops at missions and schools before arriving at Kerema air-strip. It was overcast and drizzling slightly. The small station of Kerema had a sawmill, and the smell of damp sawn wood hung in the air. The earth was rust-red underfoot.

From the air-strip I travelled up-river in a narrow, hollowed-out palm tree of a canoe with a great outboard motor on the back. It's easy to get lost on these great rivers – one waterway branching off to left or right looks very much like another. The scenery never varies, and it's hard to judge distance. Korevake village sat high on the banks of the river, and a group of children waved cheerfully from the shore. I picked my way inexpertly across the tethered rolling logs that made up the village mooring and scrambled up the bank. Kingfisher-blue butterflies the size of birds hovered over the great red ginger plants as I walked along the grass path from the river to the village. The huts here were raised on stilts high above the ground, and some had different-colour leaves or cane woven into the walls for decoration.

Stan took me to meet my family. Mai had one son and four beautiful daughters, and this was her problem. Her husband wanted her to bear him another son; one was not enough. Mai said she thought she was thirty-eight: she looked fifty. Sago production is a physically exhausting process; that and child-bearing had taken their toll. Her teeth had gone through chewing betel-nut – the only pleasure available to her – and sitting on the river bank out of her husband's earshot she confessed that she was too tired to go on child-bearing. 'Too much pain,' said Mai, rubbing her abdomen. She had heard that somewhere down the river she could have her tubes tied, but how to leave the gardens, the cooking and her family and travel down river without the knowledge of her husband?

At thirty-eight Mai was already at the end of her life expectancy. I adored her, and we spent cheerful mornings sitting at the top of the steps of a neighbour's hut while the women initiated me into chewing betel-nut. They gossiped endlessly about their husbands and the sexual antics of various white males who had come through the village and the region and left their marks – one of them in the shape of a pretty, dark-skinned girl with fine blonde curls. Her father was a German, confided Mai, spitting betel-juice expertly through the slatted floor. The mother was a village girl who had gone to find her man in town. She had stayed on there as a house-girl, making a better living than she could have done in the village. I nodded, salivating feebly, and one of the women handed me a blue plastic beaker to dribble into. 'Em spark, missus?' she asked sympathetically, combing her fingers through my hair, much admired for its straightness.

Betel starts by drying your mouth out so it feels like cardboard, then you start to salivate furiously and have to get rid of the bright-red juice. Betel brings on a light-headed, slightly euphoric feeling – the spark – even the giggles.

Mai took me to the swamps at the side of the river where the women prepared the sago. It was the hardest and the most smelly work I had ever seen. They stood deep in the stinking black mud avoiding sharp, vicious sago thorns which grow as long as six inches all the way up the bark of the tree. Although men fell the palm, strip the outer bark and hack out the pith, the rest is women's work. The pith has to be kept damp by pouring bucket after bucket of water on it while the women beat it to a pulp with a metal pipe which they twirl around their shoulders and over their heads as stylishly as American cheerleaders. The pith slides down a chute and into a bucket.

It takes about a day to beat an entire trunk to a fine powder, which starts out pale pink but becomes deeper in colour the longer it's exposed to the air. After a day or so the sago turns an extraordinary henna orange. There are all sorts of taboos attached to foods in Papua New Guinea, and some very particular ones surrounding the quality of sago and who is allowed to prepare and cook it. The deeper the colour of the sago the better the quality is reckoned to be, and the deeper-red sago must never be beaten by girls who have not yet menstruated.

The heat, smell, flies and mosquitoes made the swamp oppressive, and I was glad to get back to the village.

It's hard to determine how sago ever came to be part of the subsistence diet in the Purari Delta, although villagers had told Stan's colleague, Simon, a tale of men from the sky throwing down some young palms, which rooted.

There was a pitched battle between skymen and earthlings after the earthlings cut the palms down. However, during a respite, the leader of the skymen explained to the Chief the uses of the sago palm, and they lived happily and prosperously ever after.

In addition to sago, which the women baked or ate like dumplings dropped into stews, there were mud crabs and shellfish to be gathered, fish to be caught, and even sago grubs – big, fat, white caterpillar-like creatures, full of protein, although off-putting to look at – to be collected. Even so, Stan said, adults and children alike were getting insufficient protein for their needs.

I remembered Alison's husband, Jay, also a nutritionist, telling me in Madang, 'every woman in PNG is under-nourished in some way. Menstruation sometimes doesn't happen till they are seventeen or eighteen years old. As soon as the reproductive capacity starts, the period goes – if it ever really arrived in the first place. Continued pregnancy and lactation mean a woman may have had only ten periods at thirty-five years old. Do you know,' he said, 'I've had women come to me and say they must be ill because they are bleeding from the vagina.'

One morning, walking between the huts on my way to Mai's, I noticed that everyone still had their woven shutters battened down and there was no Mai pottering around outside exchanging gossip with her neighbours. I found her inside, cooking sago sticks over hot ashes on a tin tray. The shutters were laced shut and weighted down by lumps of wood. She put a finger to her lips and rolled her eyes shut. 'Shhh,' she said. 'Bad spirits. They were out last night, in the village.'

Although nobody wanted to talk about it much, the other women corroborated Mai's story: there *had* been bad spirits about last night. I was told to be careful walking through the village at night – I might get attacked by someone mistaking me for an evil spirit. 'Make sure you carry a torch with you if you're out, and don't stray off the main village path,' one of the men said.

Nearly all Papua New Guineans believe in some kind of sorcery and witchcraft. Certainly river-dwellers do. I've often thought that if I lived at the side of one of these great rivers I would too. Once, staying on a ridge high above the Karawari River, I lay listening to the strange-sounding calls and noises floating up from the river-banks. I was sharing a hut with an Australian who had lived here many years. 'Christ!' he said, as another wail pierced the night, 'It's so bloody black it makes no difference if you open your eyes – you still can't see a bloody thing!'

One night, returning from the precarious toilet arrangements of a hut with a hole in the floor built high on stilts out in the river, reachable only by a frenzied dash up two slender branches placed over mud and shit, balancing toilet-roll and torch, I saw a mass of lights in front of me. It was a windy night and, as the breeze blew, so too did the lights. They were like a giant diamond necklace weaving and dancing – or even Christmas decorations. As I got closer to the village, I saw that the lights were in a tree, the branches swaying and bending against the night sky. I stood with my mouth open for minutes, mesmerized, before I realized they were fireflies.

Far to the north-west of the Purari Delta, across the Star Mountains and the Central Range, is the source of Papua New Guinea's greatest river, the Sepik. Starting high in these mountains, close to the border with Indonesia, before plunging down to the wetlands and lakes, the Sepik River is the heartland of Papua New Guinean art and culture, with its great spirit houses, storyboards and masks. At the side of the Chambri Lakes mist spun around the tree-tops like great spiders' webs. Lush valleys stretched below. There was a strange reflection, and I realized that these weren't valleys at all but one vast swampland covered in brilliant-green floating weed that looked solid enough to walk on.

Near the source of the Sepik, in the Central mountains,

are scattered the Min people, who believe themselves to be the children of Afek.

When Afek arrived from the east, says the legend, she was carrying a string-bag. It fell to the ground, and the things that fell out were the beginnings of life. The string-bag, or bilum, is now Papua New Guinea's unofficial emblem, alongside its official one, the bird of paradise.

One of the bravest people I knew in PNG, as well as one of the most creative, was a tiny blonde photographer teaching at the National Arts School. Maureen Mackenzie travelled round the country fearlessly. She spoke pidgin perfectly and made many Papua New Guinean friends in the most inaccessible places, studying the meanings behind the patterns and colours used in their body decoration. Then she embarked upon a massive piece of research, writing a thesis on the symbolism and meaning of bilums.

Every part of the bilum has meaning: the colour, the weave, the decoration. The women wear them from their heads and down their backs, and close inspection will reveal children, vegetables, pigs, betel-nut, even small dogs inside, though not all at the same time. Alongside the everyday, functional bilums there are the sacred bilums. Only men have access to these, and they are kept in the men's houses, inaccessible to foreigners and women. These bilums are the means by which the initiated can gain access to their ancestral spirits. Those who look after these sacred bilums refer to themselves as 'cowboys', and are proud of their bravery and willingness to take on dangerous spirits. Some of these ritual bilums might carry the remains of a dead warrior or a bone of a promiscuous woman to ensure sexual success.

One man told Maureen, 'The bilum is like our car and our workshop. It is like your books in a library. The bilum is the mother of us all. If you haven't got a good bilum you won't be able to dance well. . . . The bilum is the road to make the bird of paradise feathers bounce up and down so that they flash and shimmer. If you haven't got a good bilum to put the bird of paradise feathers on to, it's hard to dance well.'

The concept of knowledge being magic, and of those with access to knowledge having access to magic, is one of the things that has led to most misunderstandings between Europeans and Papua New Guineans. Cargo cults were a part of that process. Under the Australians, cargo cults were illegal, and leaders or followers of a cult could be imprisoned for six months. Cults still sprang up, though, many directly political. The locals believed the Europeans were deliberately witholding knowledge from them, so there were always leaders looking for ways to release the captive spirits who would make the goods, or cargo, available.

Resentment against the European's refusal to share their knowledge erupted in a bizarre incident in 1953, when two young Australian patrol officers were killed in one of the most brutal acts of violence that had ever taken place against whites in New Guinea. With the benefit of hindsight, the reasons for its happening are only too understandable.

In October 1953 the villagers in the mountainous Telefomin area in the north-west, towards the Indonesian border, decided that they had had enough of the Australian Administration and that one way of getting rid of it would be to wage a war. In a society used to tribal wars, it probably seemed the obvious and logical way to make the Australians leave. The victims, Leo Szarka and Gerald Harris, hadn't been in the territory long and had been in the Telefomin district for no time at all. They were carrying out a census patrol when they were killed and parts of Szarka's body were ritually eaten. Had it been an age and a country of more efficient communications, the Szarka and Harris murders would probably have reverberated world-wide; as it was, the affair only just opened up a can of worms that the Australians would have preferred to keep the lid on. The administration of the country, and certainly of the Telefomin district, showed that, far from being benevolent latecomers to the colonial stage and leading the world in 'enlightened native administration', some Australians were aggressive colonial masters and pretty bloody awful at it.

Probably the most extraordinary thing about the Szarka–Harris killings was the frankness with which the local murderers admitted their intentions to the crime. One of the murderers, a village headman called Kornsep, said another came to him to ask his opinion. According to a witness, Kornsep said, 'Novonengim said "the Kiap is always attempting to destroy us, so I have come to you. I would like to kill the Kiap but I would like to hear what you have to say first." ' (A Kiap is a patrol officer.)

There had been repeated warnings brought to Telefomin that the natives intended to attack the station. Letters from Leo Szarka to his parents indicate that the administration had been both racist and violent, and the files in the archive detailing the crime itself and the subsequent hunt for the murderers make gruesome reading. Through official memos, pencilled notes and radiograms you can sense the tension building up between Port Moresby and Canberra, the seat of the Administration and the Department of Territories.

After setting out on patrol, for some inexplicable reason Szarka divided his party into two, separating himself from Harris.

The witnesses' statements are baldly detailed:

At Misinmin the Kiap went to the rest house. He had a canvas chair which folded up. The Kiap went down near the village to sit in the sun. He sat down and opened up a village book. When the Kiap sat down to census only Constable Buritori was with him. The Kiap's cook-boy had gone to wash some clothes. Some of the carriers were away collecting firewood and others were drawing water.

The Kiap opened the book ready to start calling the names of the people when two of the men came forward towards the Kiap. They were the two headmen. They came up to the back of the Kiap. They did not stand up near the Kiap but went right up to him and grabbed the Kiap round the neck and pulled him backwards out of the chair on to the ground. He struggled free from the two headmen and ran away towards the bush. He was caught again.

After he had been literally hacked to death Szarka's belongings were distributed among the villagers:

They gave everybody something belonging to the Kiap and threw the rest away in the bush. Then they killed a pig, cut it up and carried the pig and the Kiap's things to the bush. There they ate the pig and the Kiap's chest, liver, arms and the flesh from his legs in one of the gardens. Before they left the village they threw the Kiap's [remains] into the latrines. I do not know where they threw the Kiap's head, but I think it was thrown in the Irip River. I did not see any of these happenings. I was told everything I have said by a man called Novonengim who is the Headman of Okfekamsan.

Harris's murder was less violent. He had been attacked while still sleeping, and after the attack his body was carried to the station by friendly villagers. One of his constables administered penicillin to him, but he died that evening.

Dissatisfied with what they perceived as a lack of openness on the part of the Administration as to the nature of their son's death, Szarka's parents threatened to make their son's letters public. Perhaps because they had never had to cope with a killing like this before, the Administration and the Department of Territories bungled its handling, even attempting to dissuade Szarka's parents from going to New Guinea for the trial. Understandably, Mr and Mrs Szarka assumed that either the Administration or the Department of Territories had something to hide, and in a way they did – the manner in which Szarka had been killed. Mr and Mrs Szarka wanted to know just how their son had died. The Administration didn't want to tell them. Mrs Szarka was told that the attack was by tomahawks, by a large number of natives, and that the body had been mutilated. When she asked if the whole of the remains were intact, she was told that no precise details were available. An interdepartmental memo between the Department of Territories and the Administration records:

> The mother – aghast – questioned each step by which Mr Marsh endeavoured to convince her that a significant portion of her son's body is contained in the coffin buried in Rockwood Cemetery. She did not accept that the full details have been withheld to spare their feelings.

Frustrated, Mr Szarka hinted that they knew enough to discredit the Administration if he chose to go public. Worried, the Administration started to investigate the allegations contained in Szarka's letters.

On one occasion Szarka had written:

> There are some 27 natives in gaol here and I have spent most of the day sorting out where they come from. The previous officer here had no Court powers so he kept them until someone could hear the case. . . . So much for the white man's prestige. I am learning more about the dictatorship of the previous officer here who should be in gaol.

Another time, he wrote:

> The reason I was pulled out of Green River so suddenly was that the Patrol Officer I relieved here had been having trouble with his police due to the fact that he was living with a native woman in the house. It was embarrassing to feel the contempt they had for him.

During the trial, each defendant was specifically asked whether the local district officer's relationship with the local woman had any bearing on their attitude to the

Government. Each was emphatic that it didn't. However, an accident in which several villagers had been drowned carrying out work on behalf of the Administration, for which compensation had not been paid to the dead men's families, was a different matter and caused much more unrest.

The death penalty was pronounced on the murderers. In London, the London Missionary Society and the Anti-Slavery Society were vociferous in opposing it. The Administration sought the views of a former Administrator. It was, perhaps, his statement as much as anything else which got the death sentence commuted to ten years hard labour. He said:

> . . . to the men now convicted and to most of their people the Administration was an armed aggressive force bringing strange new laws and responsibilities. It is said that our very presence interfered with their crops and gardens and, much as I regret to say it, some of our past actions could be classed as unduly aggressive and, in most instances, thoughtless. The Eliptamins beat us to the punch in the only way they knew.

Years later, on a frosty night in Australia, Maureen Mackenzie and I were sitting toasting ourselves in front of a log fire and I mentioned how fascinating I found the case.

'Oh, I met a couple of those guys,' said Maureen. 'They were really matter-of-fact about it. They explained to me how the Australians had asked to see their magic. So they took them into the men's house and showed them the sacred bilums. In return, the Aussies had offered to show the Telefomin their magic, but they didn't. They didn't understand that what they had seen in the men's house was sacred. They laughed at them and wouldn't show their magic.' She sighed, 'The Aussies just didn't understand.'

★

High in the Star Mountains, on the border with Irian Jaya, sits another piece of magic: Ok Tedi. Ok Tedi is probably the best-known and most infamous of all Papua New Guinea's mines; it represents all of Papua New Guinea's potential and all of its problems. The site of the mine, Mount Fubilan, is a 6600 ft peak of copper ore with a gold capping. The Star Mountains were not really accessed until 1957, and until the mid-1980s there were virtually no roads – you either walked or flew in. There were no schools, clinics or health patrols, and hardly any mission influence. Malaria is hyperendemic and the life expectancy of the local people is between thirty and forty years. The Wopkaimin, on whose land the magic mountain stands, number less than eight hundred.

The Wopkaimin were never seriously consulted when the Australian Administration first granted prospecting rights in 1969. Originally a marginalized community of horticulturist hunters trying to scratch a living from unproductive land, they now, to a certain extent, hold some power, but at what price?

The massive influx of Western technology has created social, political, economic and cultural changes, and the Min peoples have been pitched headlong into a cash economy, reduced from a position of mastery over their small-scale traditional society and culture to being somewhat important but virtually powerless pawns within an incomprehensibly large game.

Tabubil is a company town established to service the mine. There are mobile bars, and shanty towns have grown up. The Ok Tedi River has become biologically dead. Heavy metals such as iron, copper, lead, zinc and mercury found in the hair of the locals show their exposure to pollution. The lack of employment opportunities led to blocking of the air-strip and the slashing of tyres. The mining company employed a private security force, desperate to keep out anyone who might cause trouble. Some Southern Highlanders who walked through the wet and cold mountains to look for work were jailed for a year. The town is set up in a way that accentuates the economic and racial differences. An Australian will be earning between A$30,000, with a further A$14,000 overtime, together with his air ticket home, while Papua New Guineans are on something like A$120 for two weeks' work and sleeping in dormitories.

Between Madang and the Highlands there are deposits of chrome, nickel and cobalt. There are timber and gas and oil. The early 1990s should see a resources boom the like of which has not been seen outside the Klondike, or Papua New Guinea's own first gold rush.

Waiting between planes at the airport at Mount Hagen, I got talking to an Israeli girl, Nava, who had been holidaying in the Sepik region. With hours to wait, we hitched a lift into town together. Mount Hagen market is one of the brightest and best in Papua New Guinea. The bus put us down at a large wire gate. Spread wide under the shade of casuarina trees, the brightly coloured bilums were laid out like vivid fishing-nets in front of the small Highland women. Some of the women smoked tobacco in thumb-size twists of old newspaper. Mounds of brightly coloured wools and nylon were piled high in front of them. Mount Hagen market has always looked richer than the coastal or Sepik markets, probably because what tourist trade there is comes to the Highlands, even if only to change planes there. Vegetables had always grown there too – potatoes and beans, even cabbage. Visitors from the Highlands were most welcome when they bought green vegetables or Irish potatoes with them to Moresby.

Nava and I walked down the wide tarmac road leading into town. Buses and Land Cruisers hurtled past. Hagen looked new and affluent. There were nasty, square, low-rise buildings of glass and tubular plastic, and the shops sold pop and video cassettes, bolts of material, and enamelled painted dishes for cooking. Outside the bank, which was packed to overflowing, two old men approached us and offered to sell their ceremonial pigs' tusks. There was a time when they would never have parted with them, but now they offered us arrows and spears too. They hung around the shopping arcades, waiting for anyone who was not a local. At the Hagen Park Motel, a guard sat behind an insurmountable wire fence.

'It may be a golden cage,' said Nava, 'but it's a cage all the same.'

Nava's father was attempting to restructure Papua New Guinea's health programme. 'The areas that need money aren't getting it,' said Nava. 'He wants to know how Papua New Guinea is so rich yet the people so poor.'

It was a hot and sunny afternoon. the Western Highlands shimmered hazily in the distance, and the air was clear. A small crowd had gathered in the road outside the tubular-plastic shopping arcade. Two men were having a fist fight outside the pastry shop. 'Have yourself a merry little Christmas,' warbled Bing Crosby.

Chapter 2

TAHITI

ANOTHER SIDE OF PARADISE

A lthough the most magical way to arrive at any South Pacific island is by sea, the opportunities to do that are now few and far between. But there's a kind of magic in flying too. Approaching Tahiti, high above the clouds, a flaming tropical dawn light slashed across the sky. As we dropped down through black clouds to circle the twin volcanic peaks of Moorea, flying low across Papeete's bay, a rainbow arced over the lagoon, framing the island, and a clear white surf crashed against dark turquoise sea.

Legend has it that Moorea is the remains of a volcano, half of which had sunk into the sea. Spirits broke off the other half – Moorea – in order to carry it away. But time was short and daybreak came, so they were obliged to let go still in sight of Tahiti's harbour. We should be glad that they did – one of the nicest things about Tahiti is the ever-changing light on Moorea's peaks across the bay.

In the airport, even at dawn, an American tourist was gyrating horribly with a beautiful Tahitian girl whose black hair hung way below her elegantly swaying bottom. Somebody put a small, strongly scented white flower behind my ear – a tiare, the national flower – while two gendarmes, bearded and kepied, stood looking on, bored. The rain pattered softly down outside.

French Polynesia has little and yet everything of the South Seas about it: the Riviera set against a backdrop of great jagged volcanoes, fertile valleys and necklaces of turquoise reefs; the Club Med transferred to paradise. The French explorer Bougainville, when he came here, confident that he had at last found the Garden of Eden, named it New Cythere, after Venus's birthplace. Later, many of France's wandering sons were to come in search of Rousseau's 'noble savage' and unspoilt paradise. The most famous of them all, of course, was Gauguin. But he was by no means the first painter to have searched for his own private paradise in this part of the world: from the end of the seventeenth century, various European painters had been painting Tahitians, and by the time Gauguin arrived there were even Americans photographically recording a way of life they knew would be soon extinct. They still kept coming, though. Herman Melville jumped ship here, and after Melville came Pierre Loti, Robert Louis Stevenson, Jack London, Rupert Brooke.

In the deteriorating splendour of Princess Pomare's old palace, I sat eating croissant and baguette from the local patisserie and drinking strong black Tahitian coffee. The Hotel Tahiti had seen better days, but it had the most beautiful frangipani tree I had ever seen. The petals started crimson at the edges and changed slowly to a deep gold at the centre. The underside of the flower was a deep sugar-almond pink. There was not a leaf on the tree, just blazing pink blossoms. It hung suspended over the lagoon, between blue sea and bluer sky.

A cockroach teetered around the rim of the breakfast table, its feelers waving wildly in the air, avoiding the waiting jaws and claws of several cats. They congregated in packs, a rag-tag bunch, one with a leg missing, several with little more than half a tail. Two of them each had an eye missing, which made me wonder if they were some kind of Tahitian breed or if there was a particularly dirty fighter among them. In the bar, French and Polynesians drank pastis and Poire William, and ageing and unsmiling ladies, their hair drawn back into tight chignons, a frangipani flower tucked decoratively behind one ear, served *blanquette de veau* and *moules marinière*. A trio of kittens played hide-and-seek across the very large and bare foot of a Polynesian.

On the plane over I had sat next to a young Frenchman on his way to New Caledonia to look for a job. He was an accountant. French Polynesia being overseas *départements*, or overseas territories, of France and its citizens being French citizens, it would be no hardship for Eric to find work there. If only Nouméa were Polynesian instead of Melanesian, he said, then it would truly be paradise.

'You know,' Eric said, 'I met a man who came here thirty years ago for a holiday and never left. He lives on Moorea now. Every so often he says that he should go back to France, but when he gets to thinking about it there's so much to do. What would he do with his house? What about the car? So he keeps putting it off. He's been putting it off for thirty years.'

'If I should ever find life too hard – really hard –' Eric said thoughtfully, 'then I should go to the Marquesas.'

The Marquesas are part of French Polynesia, a remote archipelago more than six hundred miles north-east of Tahiti. The locals call them the Land of Men. These were the islands where Gauguin was to flee to after the horrors of Tahiti and where Herman Melville jumped ship. Melville wrote two books about the Tahitian islands: *Typee* and *Omoo*. In both he castigated the missionaries and spoke out against the ruination of the islands – this in 1842. Cook had foreseen the spoiling of the islands almost one hundred years earlier.

When Gauguin arrived here, in 1891, Tahiti's capital, Papeete, was commercial and European, a stopover for whalers and traders – hardly the Arcadian paradise he was seeking. It's uncertain how Gauguin originally decided on Tahiti, but it's probable that he stopped off there during his days as a merchant seaman. He was caught up in the social whirl as soon as he arrived. The cost of living in Papeete didn't come cheap even then, and Gauguin wavered between relishing the calmness and stillness of tropical nights and the warmth and beauty of the Polynesians and being appalled by the impact of Western culture and disease. It wasn't long before he decided to leave the capital and travelled round the south coast of the island to settle at Mataiea. At least the locals there still lived to a certain extent as they had always done – in thatched huts, fishing in the lagoon, hunting wild boar on the steep slopes of the mountains. The eighteen months Gauguin spent there were probably his only happy time; it was also a creative time when he produced his best Tahitian work and lived with his thirteen-year-old wife and model, Teha'amana.

Papeete's back streets in the Chinese quarter still have a few wooden-frame buildings, and with a giant step of the imagination, and an even more giant step back from the modern shore-front, I tried to conjure up the town as it must have looked a hundred years ago. It was hard going: too many Peugeots on the road; '*Buvez Coca-Cola*' shrieked at me from the side of a building. The photographs in the estate agents' windows were selling land here and even encouraging Papeete's senior citizens to spend the remainder of their days in Rabuka's Fiji. France's Prime Minister had just presented the Major General with the *Légion d'honneur*.

In a poky office on the corner of a narrow street I haggled with a Chinese called Robert – much rolling of the R – over the cost of hiring a car. I wanted to drive round the south shore to where Gauguin had lived. Robert drove a hard bargain. A single, long wisp of hair emerged from his chin. His French, tinged with Chinese, was twangy and hard to get used to. 'Don't worry about the petrol,' he said airily with a wave of the hand – 'driver's responsibility.' The fuel-gauge read 'Empty' as I roared out of Papeete – like Toad, glad to be on the open road.

It had been raining since I arrived, and the Pacific was grey and unlovely. The sea crashed viciously on to the shore. There was not a soul to be seen, and the windscreen wipers seemed to be working at half-speed, unable to clear the pelting rain from the glass. Along the island's southern shoreline nestled rich villas in coconut groves, behind high hedges and gardens cultivated with bougainvillaea and frangipani. The French here were obviously very rich and very comfortable. I couldn't see the ocean, and I missed the raggle-taggle of thatched huts and straggling villages that are the mark of real Pacific islands. Small shopping plazas and modern *supermarchés* lined the road instead of open markets or women selling their home-grown mangos and papaya under the trees.

I finally found the Gauguin museum at the end of the botanical gardens. I knew that his original, palm-thatched home had not survived the ravages of the tropical climate, ocean winds and insects, but I had expected some feeling of what it might have been like – a view, a garden, something. Inside the low, modern white building was a sad little exhibition that consisted of photographs and prints of the Gauguins that existed all over the world except in Tahiti. Russian and American museums topped the list; the French were runners-up. Even Czechoslovakia and Finland boasted originals, but Tahiti owned none. In a side room I came across three originals, two of them on permanent loan. One was of a northern-French, poplar-lined road; one a portrait of Gauguin's children; the third from Brittany days, I think – *Le Sabotier*, 'The Shoemaker'. In a glass case were a couple of carved wooden spoons and a wooden bowl. The museum had done its best. All round the walls were long texts and photographs of paintings to guide you through the reproductions. I stood in the rain and tried hard to envisage something a little less like Kew. Intruding into the corner of my eye was 'Le Snack' and a chic boutique selling tie-dye pareus, straw hats and picture-postcard Gauguins.

When Somerset Maugham came here to research *The Moon and Sixpence* he was lucky enough to come across a nearby hut where Gauguin had once stayed. While there, Gauguin had painted three wooden doors, a thank-you to his host. By the time Maugham got to them the owner's children had almost scraped away the paintings, but he managed to rescue one of the panels and ship it back to France. Just before he died, Maugham's art collection was auctioned at Sotheby's. The door fetched more than $37,000, which wasn't a bad profit: he had paid the Polynesian landlord 200 francs for it.

Gauguin wrote his own book, *Noa-Noa*, about the islands. Translated from the Polynesian, 'noa-noa' means 'fragrance' or 'perfume'. *Noa-Noa* is part autobiography – Gauguin's own portrait in words and woodcuts of his life in Tahiti – punctuated with Tahitian legends. The legends were supposedly told him by his child bride, Teha'amana, but Gauguin had earlier been lent a book, *Voyages aux Îles du Grand Ocean*, written by a Belgian, J. Moerenhout, and Gauguin borrowed freely from this. *Voyages aux Îles du Grand Ocean* is two large volumes chronicling Polynesian customs and Tahitian religions, together with insights into Polynesian beliefs, languages and social structures. The book had been published in Paris over fifty years earlier, although Gauguin apparently didn't see it until he was living in Tahiti.

In *Noa-Noa* Gauguin writes of his marriage to the young Polynesian, Teha'amana. He was, of course, still married to his Danish wife, Mette. Both relationships were, at the least, unsatisfactory. The relationship with the Polynesian girl was both unequal and unfair, as indeed was his relationship with Mette. The first to heap scorn on the heads of missionaries and colonialists for their exploitation of the locals, Gauguin behaved exactly the same. When he returned from a trip to Paris with syphilis, Teha'amana understandably refused to have anything more to do with him. Undaunted, he soon found himself another young companion.

Gauguin was away from Tahiti for two years, and when he returned he was appalled by the changes that had taken place. He found Papeete more commercial and more colonized than ever. His syphilis was taking over, and he was in and out of hospital for long periods at a time. He even attempted suicide, but vomited the arsenic up

Last-minute additions to a Papua New Guinean girl's face decoration or bilas.

Papua New Guinean children in bilas, decorated with cowrie shells and bird of paradise feathers.

One of a series of buildings, scattered along the ocean shore, which make up
Bengt Danielsson's home on Tahiti.

The *Tamarii Moorea* at the Moorean waterfront, Tahiti.

A stone tiki on Tahiti.

again. His output of paintings had reduced and, in order to make ends meet, he took a job in the public works department. Then – the answer to every artist's prayer – a Parisian art-dealer offered him a regular financial arrangement which enabled him to move away from the capital to the distant Marquesas. By now his health and eyesight were both failing.

Despite the remoteness of the archipelago, here too he was disappointed. He wrote of the impossibility of finding the kind of carvings and sculptures the locals used to make. 'The gendarmes have stolen them', he said, despairingly, 'and sold them to collectors.' The old Gauguin still shone, though. He built himself a house, which became known as The House of Pleasure, and this time took a fourteen-year-old companion.

By the time Gauguin had reached Tahiti, any remains of Polynesian history, religion or temples had already been destroyed on the orders of the missionaries. The church also refused him a Christian burial, and some of his works were burned as indecent and profane. Any form of pilgrimage to Gauguin's burial place would be a test of devotion for even the most faithful acolyte. An occasional copra boat stops there on its way round the islands, but the service is infrequent. The once-weekly flights are booked up months in advance, and it takes as long to fly to these unspoilt, outer islands of French Polynesia as it does to cross the Atlantic. The journey would also prove fruitless, for today nothing remains of his houses or his art.

★

Another famous son of Tahiti, very much alive, and living on the south coast, is a tall, polite Swede called Bengt Danielsson. Danielsson arrived in Tahiti aboard the *Kon Tiki*, the papyrus raft that Thor Heyerdahl sailed from Peru to Tahiti. Heyerdahl had set out on a journey that still looks slightly mad today. He was determined to prove his thesis that the Sun-God ancestor of Peru was the same Tiki, Son of the Sun, from whom the Eastern Pacific islanders claim they are descended. Heyerdahl and Danielsson met in Peru, where Danielsson, an anthropologist who was studying the mountain Indians, said he'd be interested in joining the expedition.

Today, Danielsson lives on Tahiti with his elegant French wife, Marie-Thérèse, and a series of cats in buildings scattered alongside the ocean shore. They are vociferous campaigners against the French nuclear tests in the Pacific, and it is on the Danielssons that visitors needing to know a little more about the island politics home in. A surprisingly tall man, Danielsson had lost none of his Swedish accent in the twenty and more years he had been living on the island. In *The Kon Tiki Expedition*, Heyerdahl describes Danielsson with affection and respect and makes reference to the fact that the only things he took with him on the voyage were as many books as the raft would stand. Old habits die hard, and we met in a building on the edge of the ocean that is his work-room and library. Bookshelves lined the walls, and, on tables and desk, magazines, periodicals, academic journals and clippings were stacked perilously high. From the window, framed by the low-hanging branches of a great shade tree, my eye was drawn across the bay to Moorea. As the light changed, so too did the shadows and colour of the island. It was a sight that must lift Danielsson's soul every time he raises his head from his work.

It was to Polynesia that France moved her atomic-testing programme in the early sixties, when the Algerians became independent. Up to then, tests had been carried out in the Sahara. Although France always knew she was not part of the superpower race, successive French governments were happy to become something that has been described as a 'lesser world power'. The French are viewed with scepticism and distrust throughout the Pacific: the worst of all the Pacific powers, least favourite nation. The *Rainbow Warrior* affair[1] didn't help their shabby image as colonizers hanging on in the face of independence all round them, at the same time as continually destroying coral reefs, fishing grounds, atolls and ocean.

Intrigued by France's aggressively secretive pro-nuclear stance in the face of *glasnost*, I asked Danielsson why he thought the French still pursued their testing with such fervour and secrecy deep down below the waters of the Pacific ocean, destroying reefs, marine life and the possibility of making a living for so many Tahitian islanders.

'It is as though the whole of the Pacific is seen by the French as an El Dorado of the future to be tapped into,' answered Marie-Thérèse. 'It can hardly be viewed as strategic.'

'Look at the size of the area they control,' said Danielsson. 'The ocean surface alone makes France a world power. It's akin to the role of the Russians in Armenia or Estonia or Latvia.'

'It was a colony, you know, that was never truly colonized – well, not until 1963, when the French army took over,' he said. 'Many of the French that arrived in French Polynesia arrived chastened by their colonial experiences in Indo-China and Algeria. They were determined to try and relive something of the old life. That was when the real colonization started. They were determined to make all of Polynesia French.'

And they did. They bought land and imposed their entire administrative system upon the islands, so that local custom and law have been entirely replaced by French.

'Before 1963,' said Danielsson, 'a Polynesian made a living from a little copra, some land and from the lagoon. He had total security.' He sighed: 'Now there are real economic problems.'

Leaning back in his chair, he said, 'People don't like the word, but I'll use it all the same: with the introduction of capitalism or, if you prefer, a European type of capitalist economy, this is what they've been dragged into. When the French started to install their nuclear programme here, they recruited from the remoter Tuamotus – islanders who had land and no real need for the work. Today Fa'a

suburb has more immigrants than Papeete and they're all
from the Tuamotus. Before the tests began, the economy
was stable; today it's not.'

Marie-Thérèse said gently, 'Nobody cares, that's all.
The French never really understood the Polynesians. The
successive French Governments have never really had a
policy for these islands. If we ask for independence, we get
money. And it doesn't matter whether the Government is
from the right or the left – it doesn't change anything. All
the Governments have had the same military policy.'

The French imposition of their own land laws explained
why I had yet to see a Polynesian village intact. Land
throughout the Pacific islands has always been something
that is held in lease, passed on through generation after
generation. It is not a commodity to be bought and sold.
Now the old custom law pertaining to land has been
replaced by French law, and so the French metropolitans
can buy and own land and buy and build villas alongside
the Pacific, which makes it difficult for Polynesians to
make a living, as they had always done, from fishing or
subsistence gardening.

'For the first one hundred years,' said Danielsson, 'the
people were left in peace. Today the Polynesians are
completely lost. They are Polynesian, but their education,
which starts from the age of two, is French.'

Today the majority of Polynesians are in favour of
independence – certainly four of the five major political
parties are. This has always been completely disregarded
by the French, both in the Pacific and in France.

'They don't want to cut the branch on which they are
sitting,' said Danielsson. 'There's a lot of gerrymandering
in French Polynesian politics!'

'They gave Algeria a referendum,' said Marie-Thérèse,
'and it's time they gave one here. But when Rocard came
through a few weeks ago he said categorically *"Non"*.
There have been no public-opinion polls, no referendum
regarding the nuclear tests – probably because the out-
come would be obvious. When they ask to have a public-

opinion poll, the Polynesians are told, "But you are part of France." '

Danielsson said, 'This is very revealing of the system. This is a foreign country, but the metropolitan French come here; they set up businesses, they marry and they have kids. French policy will never be determined from here, away from France. All the decisions are being – will be – made in France.

'The Polynesians have always been rather submissive,' he added. 'They have a rather submissive attitude, although today some of the younger ones speak up. Melanesian society is and was more democratic. But here there's always been the chief and the commoner. And the commoner could never become a chief. There was never a democratic system here, so Polynesians today still hold all authority in high esteem. It's just that the French replaced the chiefs.'

Perhaps the most extraordinary effect that the French have had on Polynesia is that these French territories don't really associate themselves with the rest of the Pacific region. This is due partly to language and partly to the French atomic testing in what is almost an entirely nuclear-free zone – the Pacific. The French Polynesians are politically isolated, and they have been taught to look to France and to know more about France and Europe than about the rest of the Pacific.

I asked Danielsson what was the main direction of his work today. 'I'm a bit of an independent,' he said, pulling on his beard. 'But I'll show you something.'

He left the room and came back with a volume of the kind of encyclopedia I hadn't seen since my childhood. It was a history book, beautifully illustrated – part of a six-volume history that he had spent the last few years putting together, using Polynesian history, archives and illustrations.

'This is something I felt I could give,' he said. Then, with a smile, 'Of course they don't use it in their schools. The history that is taught in the schools is French history. But today, when the Polynesians are disoriented with their culture and identity and have lost their roots, they're becoming more and more interested in their own past. The younger ones, of course, don't know anything that happened before 1963.'

Outside the window the sun was hard and white, and Moorea's silhouette loomed black from the sea. As I was leaving, Marie-Thérèse said, 'For the Tahitians, the future is Hawaii. They love it. There are cheap fares and there is enough of Polynesia – they never feel at home in France.'

On the way back into Papeete I drove through Fa'a. Remembering what Danielsson had said, I left the coastal sprawl of villas and luxury apartment blocks that wouldn't have been out of place in Cannes or Nice and headed inland towards the foot of the mountains. The dirt roads up to the slopes of the volcano were more like South American barrios than a South Pacific island. Dark-haired children with oval eyes played in the streets outside concrete blocks of apartments. Further up the slopes of the mountain, high above the ocean, the shanty town sprawled like something from Brazil or the Caribbean. The trouble with poverty, particularly silhouetted against the golden light of a setting Pacific sun, is that it is very picturesque.

It had rained without stopping for a week, although the rains weren't due for another three months. Being a fair-weather traveller and, therefore, dispirited I took shelter in the cafés of Papeete and tried to look beyond the skyscrapers and bars of the bustling small town. But it was hard to believe I was in a paradise of sorts and not some small French port. Cute Tahitian girls wore chic denims and Bermuda shorts, and the skinny, elegant Chinese all wore designer dresses. The waterfront was lined with boutiques selling bikini bottoms and cafés with red starched table-cloths and a smell of garlic.

Everything stopped at lunchtime and France took over completely. Carafes of rosé and baskets of neatly sliced baguettes were slapped down on to tables groaning under *salade niçoise*, prawns, swordfish and *frites*. In the cafés, old men sipped pastis and coffees, and backpackers drank beer. At the local *presse* Catherine Deneuve smiled from the pages of *Elle* side by side with Fergie. In a back street there was a Conforama, part of the French supermarket chain. There was even a Euromarché, its shelves packed with terrines and *pâté de lapin*, quail's eggs, wines and aperitifs, Roquefort and Reblochon, Camembert and ropes of garlic. There was an incessant drone of French pop music, and *les traveaux* caused a traffic jam all the way in and out of town.

As I was dodging the puddles in a side-street a tall, big-boned girl in a vivid pink leotard and a tight pink T-shirt offered me shelter under her umbrella – 'Viens, cherie!' Then she called out something in Polynesian to two Chinese sheltering in the doorway of one of the local clubs. She wasn't a 'she' at all, but one of Tahiti's cheery 'third sex', a mahu or transvestite.

The mahus have always been more than openly tolerated in Tahiti, although when the missionaries first arrived they were shocked to discover that not only did the mahus exist, but also they were encouraged to do the jobs that women would normally do. They looked after children, worked as maids and cooked – all the while wearing women's clothes, or whatever they wanted. In festivals and celebrations, the mahus took the women's parts. Today's mahus work as bartenders and waiters, but how long this can go on before it turns into straightforward prostitution in a place like Papeete is anyone's guess. The nightclubs have already started to feature male striptease artists.

My friend shrieked with glee that I had come from Britain and threw his hands up despairingly at the price of ever being able to leave Tahiti for anywhere – preferably, for him, San Francisco. But only on a visit, he said. He was happy here and had no wish to go to colder climates or large cities. We shared the umbrella as far as the waterfront, and he urged that I do as the rest of Papeete did and leave the city for the weekend, particularly if I had no 'special someone worth staying for'. A vision in pink, he – she? – imperiously waved at the oncoming traffic to stop and let him through, which it did.

★

The lure of Moorea's shadow proved too much. Finally I bought a ticket at the wharf and jumped on the old car ferry that chugs regularly across to the island. Papeete looked neat and well-ordered from the sea, its mountains rising blue-green away from the sea. We sailed past the white gingerbread sprawl of the Hotel Tahiti and the crimson frangipani hanging over the lagoon. The little boat headed towards the cleft between the two great jagged peaks of Moorea.

Moorea's lagoon is probably one of the most beautiful in the world, and now the sun was beating down and the white sand beaches stretched for ever to the west. It was a blissful nothing after Papeete – no cars, no snacks, no bars, no buildings up the green slopes; just a signpost pointing to the east or the western part of the island. A newly built bus terminal kept the sun off the heads of the waiting passengers, and a cluster of wooden buses waited for business. I had no idea which way was which or where I was going. 'Prenez la jaune, la jaune', said a helpful man, pointing to a truck. So I took the yellow truck, which set off in the completely opposite direction to all the others, towards the west, through coconut groves and past the lagoon, crystalline and pure. The only other two passengers, young Polynesians carrying acoustic guitars, got off at the end of a dirt road and disappeared into a palm grove.

Where were the villages, I asked. We would get there, said the driver. A mile or so further on he stopped. 'Billy's Holiday Village' the sign read.

'No,' I said, 'a Polynesian village.'

No such thing, said the young man. I'd have to settle for the Club Med. I looked disapproving and tried to argue, but he was right: there were no villages any more. The only thatched huts belonged to the holiday villages and lagoon-side hotels. This was an island paradise of chalet bungalows, Club Med and Martha's Boutique and Snack.

Finally I jumped down at something called the Hibiscus Hotel, which at least looked local, and crept through blistering heat to have a beer. The driver agreed we would meet at the petrol pump, in time for me to take the ferry back to Papeete.

The Hotel Hibiscus was local and pleasant, and there was nobody there but me and a cat. The lagoon stretched out azure and inviting. Two boys waded out from the shore to a raft moored in the centre of the lagoon, where they somersaulted and dived and played like two dolphins. Their dog played with them, and blistering heat seared off the beach. Two Polynesian girls wearing lava-lavas hitched their skirts up, wound their hair into a knot and swam out to join them. Despite the midday heat, the dog snuggled up against them. On the beach a Polynesian family played and a man cradled a puppy in his arms, trickling cool water over its back. One of the bargirls came over with a handful of tiare flowers and put one behind my ear.

The beer was sending a buzz through my head, and the lagoon and its raft seemed a good idea in the heat, when all of a sudden the midday peace was cut into by a noise of whirring engines and low over the reef, like something out of *Apocalypse Now*, screamed a helicopter. It made several passes over the reef and landed on the beach in a storm of sand. 'Club Med,' said the bargirl smiling.

Later I headed for the local petrol pump where I was to wait for the bus. There was no sign of life anywhere, other than a mechanic pumping up a tyre.

It was getting late. I appealed to the mechanic where might the bus be.

'Gone,' he said simply.

'What do you mean "gone"? It's not quarter past yet.'

Patiently and very slowly he enunciated in French, *'Il est parti, madame.'*

73

'But he can't – it's not time.'

'No more buses,' said the Polynesian. Then, to rub it in, 'No more buses until tomorrow morning.'

'What about taxis?'

'Non.'

'Cars, to rent?'

'Non.'

'What can I do?'

He shrugged his shoulders.

'I have to get back. What' – I tried a winning smile – 'would you advise?'

'There is nothing you can do, madame. Not until tomorrow.'

'There must be a car somewhere on this island.'

He pointed at himself.

'Well,' I said, relieved.

'But it'll cost. It is not', he said firmly, 'convenient for me at this moment.'

'I don't have any choice,' I snapped.

He agreed that I didn't have a choice and named an exorbitant figure. Defeated by heat and lassitude, I agreed. We climbed into a transit van and headed off down the road. Moments later we turned into a driveway and, while his wife came to the window and smiled politely, he disappeared into the house, re-emerging in a spotless white shirt and shorts.

Further on round the island, a group of Europeans sat forlornly at the side of the road.

'You may be in luck,' said my driver. 'They've missed the bus too.' He winked. 'Less money to pay!'

'They' were a group of Australians from a camping site. The driver named his price, but they told him where to take his transit van and said they'd rather spend another night on the island. Unperturbed, he shrugged and carried on.

'You know,' I said, 'I've lived in the Pacific for several years, and in all that time I've never known any form of transport to leave early. It's unheard of – *jamais, jamais*.'

He laughed happily, as well he might.

Halfway round the island, a black-haired girl stood at the side of the road.

'Now this time you may be in luck,' he said. 'Half the fare if she's going to the ferry.'

I yelled out the window at her, and she ran down the road. Yes she was going to the ferry. Yes she had missed the bus. She had been standing at the side of the road when it drove past her, on the other side of course.

'*Logicamente*,' said Georgina, who turned out to be Mexican, '*Logicamente*, you would think the bus would come back on this side of the road, towards the ferry. So when I see it coming, I let it pass, because he has to turn at the end of the island. But no, it doesn't. And I have a plane to catch to Fiji tonight.'

'It seems to me', I said to the driver, 'that you and the bus driver could have a little business arrangement here, non?'

Both hands lifted off the steering-wheel. 'Madame, how can you say, how could you think such a thing?'

We arrived at the wharf as the *Tamarii Moorea* whooped, belched black smoke and pulled away from the waterfront, but we made it.

Sitting on the deck we sank into an ice-cold beer.

'How would you describe Papeete?' asked Georgina. 'It's *muy civilisado*.'

'Over-developed,' I said gloomily.

She laughed. 'That's a much better way of describing it.'

She sighed. 'If I want to go to France, I go to France. I came here to see the Pacific, not France.'

Georgina was in fabrics and had come to sell hand-painted Mexican goodies to the chic boutiques of the South Seas. 'And you know what they want?' – she clutched at her head distractedly. 'Even I, who comes from Mexico, even I can't wear them in this weather – denim! They all want denim!'

★

Back on Papeete's quayside, the bonito fishermen were rushing their catch to market. The solid silver-blue fish hung from arching poles slung across their shoulders, coolie-style. A Chinese family were cooking and selling *crêpes* from the back of a van. Further along from all this waterside activity bobbed the expensive and exclusive private yachts

In Samoa I'd met a yachtie who had arrived one day in the local bar from Tahiti. He told me of a notorious brothel in Papeete which boasted the most beautiful women in the South Pacific. He had gone there to see for himself – not, of course, intending to avail himself of any of the local beauties, but curious to see what and who was on offer. While there, drinking a few beers, he fell into chatting in broken French and English with one of the girls, an exquisite creature quite a lot older than he was. The next night he went back again and stayed late, chatting to her. When she went off with a client, he returned to his boat.

In the early hours he heard someone calling his name from the quayside. It was the woman, having finished her shift at the brothel. So they sat under a starry sky and drank a few beers (well, that was his story anyway), and this was repeated for several nights until it became clear to both of them that, despite language difficulties, the whole thing was becoming serious.

She didn't want him to visit her at the brothel and, because of certain shipboard arrangements, he couldn't take her aboard. So, finally, she agreed to take him back to her place. On the agreed night, however, she didn't turn up.

The next night he went looking for her, but she wasn't at work and nobody would tell him where to find her. A couple of nights later she turned up again in the early hours on the quayside, where, in floods of tears, she said she couldn't take him home because she had a small daughter there. Professing that he loved her deeply and it didn't matter and he'd come at the weekend to see her and meet her daughter and do everything the right way, they agreed she'd come to the boat at the weekend and take him home.

Yet again she didn't turn up. This time he really was beside himself, but on the Monday the same pattern repeated itself and she arrived at the quayside. Finally, in tears, she said she also had a common-law husband, French, the father of her child, who had unexpectedly come back from a trip to another island. It was obvious that the relationship would never be consummated, and so the young man sailed away and she went back to either the brothel or the husband, or both.

Well, that was the way he told it to me, and I liked the story, which I thought had a Somerset Maugham ring to it.

★

Moorea had a lot more going for it than Papeete, so I arranged to store my bags, packed a holdall and headed back for the ferry. This time on the boat dock at Vaiare I eschewed 'la jaune' and took a blue bus instead, heading in the other direction. After about half an hour's drive, and long after we had left the Sofitel and the Bali Hai behind, I asked the driver to put me down outside a small hotel with some thatched huts, at the side of the lagoon, which didn't look 'muy civilisado'.

That afternoon I borrowed a snorkel and mask from a local boy and lazed around the lagoon coral until the sun set.

That night, for the first time in too long, I lay awake listening to the booming of the ocean on the reef and remembered the first time I had slept in a thatched hut on a desert island. It had been on New Ireland, one of the Papua New Guinea islands, at a place called Lemakot. Lemakot was a maternity hospital run by an order of nuns. Built of thatch and cane at the side of the ocean, the hospital was headed by Sister Genevieve, who delivered probably the healthiest babies in Papua New Guinea. Women came from all over the island to have their babies there. As is customary, both the hospital and the adjoining buildings were raised off the ground, and I remember lying awake my first night listening not only to the crashing of ocean on reef but also to the snuffling of the local pigs beneath the slatted floor.

There were no pigs here on Moorea – only the sociable chatter of the mynah birds next morning, jumping excitedly up and down on the pandanus roof, picking their way through an insect breakfast. A mahu brought me my breakfast of papaya and coffee.

'How long are you staying?' he asked.

'Just a few days.'

'If you're here on Friday,' he rolled his eyes, 'you must come dancing. We have a club.' He minced off in a wildly hibiscus-patterned lava-lava, swinging his hips, a hibiscus behind his ear.

The club was the local community hall, but on Friday nights it became the Tabu Disco and jumped to the screams of electric guitars. I saw my friend leaving for his Friday-night bop soberly dressed in jeans and a pristine white shirt.

Later I asked him about the intricacies of paddling an outrigger canoe – how to do it without going round in ever-decreasing circles.

'Ooogh!' he squawked. 'Don't ask me! I wouldn't even go *out* in one of those things.'

'But you're Polynesian, a natural sailor. You're supposed to have an affinity for anything to do with water.'

He looked at me pityingly. 'You'd better go down the village and ask one of the boys; they know all about that stuff.'

That night even the surf was not loud enough to drown the sounds of the tropical night: electric guitars and the revving-up of thousands of tiny Vespa engines. The Tabu raved till two, and then the locals roared off home. Unable to get back to sleep, I went for a walk. The smell of the frangipani was strong and sweet, and the moon sent down a clear silver light. A young couple sat hand in hand, without speaking, gazing out across the blackness of the lagoon.

On Sunday it rained again, so I teetered off on a Vespa hired from a local kiosk and went exploring. Moorea's valleys are sweet and lush, and it was a long, winding climb up the dirt road to as far up the mountain as I could go. Once at the top, the island was swathed in mist and cloud and driving rain. In neat green meadows, black and white cows grazed happily under the shade of the mountains. I could see why Eric's friend had dithered about leaving it for the past thirty years.

The day I was due to leave, I placed myself firmly in the middle of the road twenty minutes before the bus was due. Half an hour later, broken by sun and impatience, I pleaded with the man mowing the grass at the side of the road.

'Rest assured, madame,' he said without hesitating, 'The bus will come at ten fifteen.'

'But it's twenty to eleven.'

He shrugged, then said, 'Ten forty-five, eleven, eleven fifteen – it will be here.'

At eleven there was a blast of its horn and the blue bus careered round the corner with a lady in an ornately flowered hat driving it. For the second time the *Tamarii Moorea* was toot-tooting impatiently as we hit the jetty.

Back in Tahiti, the local newspapers were splashing the headline news that, after twenty-five years, the French High Commissioner had decided that the French Polynesians had the right to be better informed about the impact of the atomic tests on their islands. A round-table discussion was being held, to which would be invited trades unions, religious leaders and environmental groups. The invitation was not, however, extended to the press. All questions raised, said the High Commissioner's office, in what was turning out to be nothing but a mammoth PR exercise, would be analysed by the Centre D'Experimentation Pacifique, the Atomic Energy Commission, and the military. The results would be later presented to the French state and the territorial government. Not until then, said the High Commissioner's office firmly, would any part of the official analysis be made public. After all, the purpose of the round table was not to create a public forum, nor indeed a forum for public debate. The Tahitian press took all this lying down, dormant, supine!

That wasn't the only interesting story. Tucked away in the pages of a local tourist handout magazine was the story of the Japanese tycoon who had just spent $75 million buying up three of Tahiti and Moorea's hotels. The tycoon, Harunori Takahashi, was to follow up his purchases with a $51 million development programme, a convention centre and golf courses. Golf courses, on Moorea's most fertile farming ground where vanilla and pineapple plantations at least provided the islanders with some kind of an economy and a link to their culture. Mr Takahashi himself was currently under investigation by the Japanese police, the Tokyo stock exchange and the Japanese Ministry of Finance for insider dealing. His international investments spread wide – London, Sydney, Saigon and Los Angeles – with holding companies in the British Virgins and the Dutch West Indies. The Territorial government, obsessed with the economic models of Hawaii and Singapore, didn't see fit to question whether Mr Takahashi's types of development model for the islands were desirable or not – let alone the sudden impact of Japanese businessmen at conventions and hotel complexes, given their appetite for the pleasures of foreign female flesh. The Japanese businessman's penchant for sex holidays could spread to French Polynesia, and the destruction of the islands would be complete.

In the Hotel Tahiti, however, life went on as normal. In scorching heat, the local French ate lunches of *lentilles aux saucisses* and *jambon salé*, with carafes of iced red wine – the kind of lunch that would floor the British in that heat. On a wooden jetty that jutted out into the lagoon, a part-

Chinese woman threw her fishing-lines out into the water. She wore a yellow hat and a scarlet lava-lava patterned with white hibiscus and was barefoot. The old lady carried a cardboard box of bread which she threw into the water. A black and white cat with a tail like a lemur purred at her side. While she fished, the cat purred and preened and wrapped himself first around her then round the box of bread. He sat patiently at her side and willed the line to yield up a fish, and his feathery tail would flick across her back with excitement every time she hauled a line in. Then, bored with the lack of results, he fell asleep in the afternoon sun.

★

It was Captain Cook who brought cats to Tahiti. Cook's Tahiti was an island of tribal wars and human sacrifices, and by the time he made his third and last journey to the islands, in 1777, the local wars and European stop-overs had already taken their toll. The Polynesians were wearing European clothing and their language was now peppered with English and French. They had taken to drink and to arms, venereal disease was spreading and, enticed by easier ways to make a living, they had stopped growing much of the local food. Cook had not discovered Tahiti – that had been done by Samuel Wallis, in charge of His Majesty's ship *Dolphin*, in 1767. At that time the island was known as Otaheite. The Otaheitians, according to Wallis, behaved amicably except that they stole everything in sight while the women did everything in their power to lure the sailors ashore. Even when the island was formally taken possession of and the British flag was run up, the outward and visible sign of the act of possession did not last long – overnight, the flagpole was stripped, and thereafter the flag was used as a dress.

After Wallis came Bougainville and after Bougainville Cook, ahead of his time in being aware of and worried by the impact the Europeans were having upon the islanders. Eleven years later in 1788 came Bligh, in the *Bounty*, on his first and notorious expedition to collect bread-fruit shoots to transport to the West Indies to feed the plantation slaves. Perhaps if Bligh had not had to wait so long, five months, before the seedlings were fit to transport, the mutiny might never have occurred. Five months is a long time, and some of the men had become attached to their women and the life-style on the island. The long journey home and its accompanying shipboard disciplines must have looked a dismal prospect, and so Bligh was set adrift on his extraordinary journey, to land, three and a half thousand miles and less than two months later, on what was then Dutch Timor, part of Indonesia.

Most of the crew, led by Fletcher Christian, went back to Tahiti before setting sail for less well charted waters but they weren't welcome. Their propensity for stealing women and livestock made them unpopular wherever they attempted a settlement and eventually they headed for the remoter Pitcairns. A group of loyal crew members stayed behind on Tahiti until taken into custody by the captain of the frigate that was sent out from England in the wake of the mutiny. The former crew members were clapped in irons while on shore, apparently, the usual Polynesian welcome was accorded to the newly arrived frigate and her crew. Of those remaining mutineers four were acquitted, another discharged, two were pardoned and three later executed at Spithead. What the sailors and the mutineers and the whalers had started, the missionaries helped to finish.

The London Missionary Society believed Christianity would be the greatest blessing they could impart to the islands and so its representatives set out for the South Seas. It wasn't a random sticking of a pin on the uncharted map of the heathen world. They had targeted the South Pacific islands after long and serious consideration, believing the states of mind and bodies of the locals, of whom they knew absolutely nothing, to be ripe material for conversion.

'May the doctrine of the cross triumph over the unparalleled obstacles it has to surmount,' one of their members wrote, 'and may it advance from shore to shore till it covers the hemisphere that is washed by the Pacific Ocean.'

And what about the natives?

'Their situation of mental ignorance and moral depravity strongly impressed on our minds the obligation we lay under to endeavour to call them from the darkness into marvellous light.' And so it was that thirty men, sixteen women and three children set sail on the expedition, among them a hatter, a stonemason, a tailor, an Indian weaver and four ordained ministers. Just what the natives needed to call them from the darkness!

The missionaries were nothing if not resolute. Their arduous journey lasted for months, from Falmouth across the Bay of Biscay to Madeira and Cape Verde, then across the Atlantic. They took on supplies at Rio de Janeiro and then sailed on to Cape Horn before heading north-west to Tahiti. On one occasion, due to bad weather, the route round the Horn had to be abandoned completely. Instead they took the eastern passage, passing south of the Cape of Good Hope, on to Australia and New Zealand. Through having to change course in this way, their voyage was lengthened by seven thousand miles. They saw only one ship after Rio and were continually seasick. The seas were 'mountain high'. But they applied themselves to learning the Otaheitian language and reading the Reverend Greathead's account of the South Sea islands to the accompaniment of spouting whales.

When the missionaries finally arrived in 1797, they hoisted out the cannons, just to show the locals who was boss. In their innocence, the Tahitians cheerfully assisted in putting the cannons on their carriages. Their helpfulness made a favourable first impression on the missionaries – but not for long. Soon their 'wild disorderly behaviour and strong smell of coconut oil lessened the favourable opinion we had formed of them,' wrote one of the brethren. It was decided to start as they meant to go on and, after the initial exuberance had died down, the missionaries held a service on the quarterdeck, where they sang, no doubt under blistering skies, 'O'er the Gloomy Hills of Darkness'. The Captain offered the King, who had paddled out in his canoe to greet them, the supreme compliment of firing the cannons. At this, the King, who was paddling round the ship while the Queen baled with half a coconut, begged them not to. The noise, he explained, was simply too great and hurt his ears.

King Pomare was a little more sophisticated than his predecessor. Having been unsuccessful in his attempts to conquer a good many of the neighbouring islands, he pragmatically came to the conclusion that the Christian God might be an effective patron and he converted to Christianity in 1812. God turned out to be on his side, and he subsequently conquered his adversaries to become King of all Tahiti. The Ten Commandments were made the legal basis for government, and all things sacred to the old religion were banned. Tattooing, singing – apart from hymns – and drunkenness were forbidden. And sex, of course. The missionaries established a morality police to supervise all matters relating to the three Ds – dress, drink and dance.

Thankfully not all the missionaries had blinkered vision and, through the journals of captains, officers and brethren aboard a series of LMS voyages, another side to the Polynesians is occasionally allowed to shine through.

'It is incredible to see the quantity of provisions poured in upon us,' wrote one. 'We have not less than a wagon-load of fruits, besides the multitudes of hogs and poultry.' The Polynesians were 'bounden in generosity to each other and to strangers, seldom retaining resentment or revenge. No person ever lifts his hand to strike a child. . . . Their dialect is the Italian of the South Sea, soft and harmonious.'

'They have in many instances more refined ideas of decency than ourselves . . .' wrote another. 'They lay the charge of immodesty at our door. Englishmen are ashamed of nothing and we have led them to public acts of indecency never before practised among themselves.'

From Tahiti, several of the brethren were to continue north-east, to the Marquesas. Here one William Crook, described as a gentleman's servant, and John Harris, a tinworker, fell into a most unchristianlike debate when Harris felt the island was too poor and the food not good enough for him. He wanted to move on, but Crook, busying himself with planning the building of a house and the cultivation of a nearby valley, was as happy as if in the Garden of Eden. One evening, when Crook was away surveying a valley, the Chief, not considering any favour too great for his two new friends, left Harris one of his wives. Harris fled to the beach in an effort to raise the attention of his shipmates, but the ship was moored too far away from shore for them to hear his cries of distress. The lady was persistent, but so too was Harris, refusing to comply with her demands. Feeling spurned, she eventually 'became doubtful of his sex' and passed this thought on to several female acquaintances. Poor Harris – the ladies arrived in the night to see for themselves what was what. Harris fled to the beach, taking his chest with him. But he was not to pass a peaceful night. At 4 a.m., regrettably true to form, yet more locals arrived, this time intent on stealing his clothes. Fearing their intentions, Harris fled to the hills.

His partner, the twenty-two-year-old Crook, stayed behind for many happy years with his medicines, garden feeds and encyclopedia.

Forty years after the British missionaries came the French missionaries. They were firmly deported on more than one occasion. It was an English missionary, George Pritchard, British Consul and adviser to Queen Pomare, who attempted to have Britain annex Tahiti. Meanwhile the expulsion of the Catholic missionaries was seen by France as a national insult, and the French took possession of the Marquesas. From there they tried to force the Queen to make Tahiti a protectorate of France. When she refused, they tried the time-honoured method of persuasion by anchoring a gunboat off Papeete and demanding an agreement that would allow the Catholics to spread the word. The English missionaries were furious, but back at home Britain was too deeply ensconced in her new territories of Australia and New Zealand to want to go to war with the French on behalf of the LMS, so Tahiti was formally annexed. Queen Pomare fled to Moorea, and for the next three years the Tahitians fought a kind of small-scale guerrilla war against the French. It was the last war they would ever wage, and to no avail. God was on the side of the big battalions.

The French penetration of Polynesia has been one of seduction rather than rape. Either way, the Polynesians have been screwed: their culture lost, their decisions made for them twelve thousand miles away in Europe. Ironically, on 14 July the islands spend two weeks celebrating the fall of the Bastille and France's revolution. Meanwhile, French culture tramples all over Polynesian culture and, rather than encourage any signs of independence, France has created a population of coffee-skinned French men and women, dependent and effectively disenfranchised.

Chapter 3

HAWAII

DISNEY COMES TO PARADISE

There was a full moon over Waikiki Beach and orchids on my pillow. The trade winds made the palm trees dance, and Hawaii had a strange mixture of beauty and profanity. The latter was more in evidence.

The orchids came with everything in Honolulu. They prettied the salads, garnished the steak and were dunked with great profligacy into some of the most vivid and vile-coloured drinks I'd ever seen. Bright-blue drinks were made even more garish, if that were possible, by the presence of small purple and crimson orchids floating on top. It seemed a terrible waste.

I hadn't particularly wanted to go to Waikiki but friends who had been there insisted. 'You've got to be in the centre of it all,' they said. I wasn't so sure.

There are eight islands in the Hawaiian group. Honolulu is the state capital, on the island of Oahu. The youngest and the largest island in the group is Hawaii itself; ironically this is the least visited. The Americans call it the Big Island. The islands are actually mountain tops, their bases deep on the ocean floor. All the islands are volcanic, although Hawaii is the only one with a currently active volcano. They have built up over the past 25 million years of eruption after eruption. Of all the islands, Maui is probably the most familiar. Lanai is one big pineapple plantation, which belongs to the Dole pineapple corporation. Niihau is owned by a family called, appropriately, the Robinsons, and is closed to anyone and everyone.

Kaho'olawe belongs to the American military and is used by them for target practice. The entire chain of islands straddles something called the Pacific plates. If these plates had been stationary, which they never have been, the entire archipelago of eight islands would be one large volcanic island.

The drive from the airport into Honolulu, alongside Hickham air-force base, through the port area and past piers, was strangely reminiscent of Gibraltar – garrison towns, perhaps. A glimpse of Diamond Head, the extinct volcano crater, in the distance made it look even more so. Then we were into downtown Honolulu – skyscraper canyons and sprawling shopping plazas. A huge mural of whales and dolphins was slowly being masked by even huger scaffolding as new buildings superseded old.

When they were the Sandwich Islands, the Hawaiian islands were the centre of the whaling trade. Now the tourists come in their hundreds to see the whales in their winter calving grounds off the islands. The result is that the whales are being driven further and further afield by the surrounding boatloads of goggling tourists, and they are today in almost as much danger as when they were hunted for their meat and oil. Anything and everything in Hawaii smacks of overkill. In the case of the whales, literally.

Surprisingly, the heart of downtown Honolulu was a sudden pleasant surprise, with a cluster of remaining graceful old buildings and the original New England mission houses regrouped together under banyan trees. The white clapboard houses had been shipped out here wholesale by the missionaries during the last century. Across the road, the Iolani Palace was a parody of Paddington lace and Palladian columns, the last reminder that Hawaii had had a flourishing monarchy before America annexed it. Today, in that uniquely American combination of hype and naïvety, it is announced as 'America's only royal palace.' There were banyans and shade trees everywhere, acacias and frangipani. I had never thought that Honolulu might be pretty, but in parts it was. Occasionally there was a tantalizing glimpse of jagged mountains, through the gaps between the sky-scrapers, and then the Pacific – an indescribable and glorious turquoise. As a child I had once had some large, Victorian glass marbles that came near it in colour. In the distance, an occasional sail moved gently across the horizon.

The colours of the ocean and a glimpse of languorous palm trees drew me through the concrete canyons, past hotels and condominiums to Waikiki Beach.

Outside the glossy lobby of the Regency Hyatt, a laughing man with a neat black beard was having trouble with the automatic roof of a bright-red convertible. At his side and in the rear seat sat two women dressed from head to foot in black. Both pairs of eyes peered out from slits in black masks – burkas – the Arab veil. I shuddered to think what these Arab women might be making of the fleshpots of Waikiki and their cult of the body.

I had never read *The Naked Ape*, but after seeing Waikiki Beach I could have contributed a chapter to it. Quite literally a human zoo, it was like a scene from one of those wildlife films where seals come on shore to take the sun and to mate. It was all display and courtship and body language. You couldn't have inserted a matchstick between the bronzed bodies spread alongside and over each other. There was not an eighth of an inch to spare.

Out at sea and performing the most extraordinary aquatic antics were the surfers. I had always envied surfers their patience and elegance, a bit like dressage in the Horse of the Year Show, with the riders of the waves drifting patiently like large sea-horses waiting for the perfect wave. I had seen that done in Australia. Here, though, were the Red Arrows of the surf. These boys stood on one leg, they twisted, they turned, they rocked and rolled, they pirouetted and raced into shore facing backwards. One golden-haired Californian type stood repeatedly on his head. It was pure show-business. They were so busy performing that they had no time to consider anyone who might get in their way. It took a brave swimmer to venture into the waves and risk concussion from the edge of a surfboard or a slice through the jugular from its fin.

A few swimmers had, however, thrown caution to the winds and tentatively splashed near the shore in an opening between two great catamarans moored to the beach. The catamarans were advertising sunset tours, sunrise tours, happy-hour tours, night tours. At the helm of one stood a bronzed young man blowing into a conch shell. He addressed himself to the swimmers, 'Get oudda da way,' he yelled. 'Woo woo,' wailed the conch mournfully. The swimmers huddled nervously in a few feet of ocean as the tourist-laden catamarans were manhandled out into the surf, at the same time as the Red Arrows came at them from the rear.

At the back of the beach, under the palm trees, a talent contest was in full swing. Fully amplified pop songs screeched across the sand, while small children and eager young men howled their way through the Top Ten. It was worse than anything I had ever imagined.

I crept back to the traffic and shoppers of Waikiki, passing on my way a wooden shelter. At a table beneath it, a group of old Japanese men sat and played cards just as they had probably done for the past seventy years, oblivious to the zoo around them.

Until then I hadn't given much thought to the Japanese families and sleekly fashionable boys and girls packed alongside all the others on the beach. Then I visited Pearl Harbor.

As a monument, Pearl Harbor and the USS *Arizona* leave a lot to be desired. There was a small museum with a few bad paintings, more interesting photographs and a bookshop stocking model kits of the *Memphis Belle* and the *Arizona*. The books were all very heroic: *Eagle Against the Sun, Heroes of Pearl Harbor, At Dawn We Slept, Target Tokyo*, and so on. There were queues everywhere. There were queues for the Coke machine, queues for plastic-wrapped sandwiches, queues for the toy aeroplanes. The queue to see the movie was followed by a queue to get on the launch that drove us out to queue to get on to the memorial. Everyone queued happily, and I queued too. The Japanese bought postcards and videoed everything and everyone.

In the cinema, a young Ranger made a little speech announcing that Pearl Harbor wasn't merely a memory or a memorial but an emotion. The Japanese looked suitably inscrutable. So did the Americans.

The documentary film of the events of 7 December 1941 was accompanied by a lot of heavenly music which, thankfully, didn't last long. The memorial itself was a kind of bridge built across the submerged midships of the *Arizona*. Only 150 bodies were ever recovered, and there are still about a thousand bodies entombed in the ship's carcass. They had died before they even knew they were fighting a war. I tried to imagine what the lines of Japanese were thinking. Perhaps they weren't. Perhaps it was easier not to.

Somewhere in the car-park, among the coaches, a lady called Marge, wearing a halo of flowers in her hair, was haranguing the homegoing customers, most of them in their sixties and seventies. Many of them had been stationed here during the war and had come to pay their respects. Some had lost friends here. They all had their memories.

Something had gone wrong with a tour-bus. 'I'm here eight hours a day trying to keep you happy,' Marge shrieked to a weary-looking group. 'What do you think it's like for me?' Nobody answered.

One of the couples crept away and joined the queue for the local bus. When it arrived, the driver was a plump woman with chopsticks in her hair and a hibiscus behind one ear. The chopsticked lady drove hell-for-leather into Honolulu as though the Japanese air force was about to take out Pearl Harbor for the second time. We arrived downtown in record time. As we got out, the elderly man turned. 'Gee lady, you're a hell of a driver,' he said, shaking his head in wonderment. His wife turned to me. 'What about that Marge?' she said, 'You know, someone should put a net over her face . . . Nice meeting you.'

I found it hard to get the image of the Japanese, queueing at the memorial to their destruction, out of my head. I'd seen it in the Solomons too, on Guadalcanal, scene of some of the bloodiest fighting in the war of the Pacific. Like old soldiers everywhere, they too have their memories of friends and lovers killed. But Pearl Harbor seemed an odd place to take the kids and video camera.

The Japanese were originally brought to Hawaii as indentured labour by the Haoles, the white plantation-owners, at the end of the nineteenth century. They came after the Chinese and before the Filipinos and the Portuguese. The Haoles had seized power and land from the original Hawaiians, who, like the Melanesians and other Polynesians, could not adapt to the monotony of cutting cane and pineapples. The notion of improving working conditions was too simple a solution for the whites; instead, they preferred to import their own acquiescent labour-force. First they brought in the Chinese, but these, sick of their bad treatment at the hands of the white foremen, promptly upped and left at the end of their contracts. They headed for Honolulu, where they successfully opened trade-stores and small businesses.

The passivity of orientals as labourers was, of course, something that existed purely in the minds of the planters, but the policy continued. Taking advantage of a bad harvest in Japan, the Hawaiian plantation owners persuaded the Japanese Government to let them import peasant farmers as contract labour from the worst-hit areas. Like the Chinese before them, the Japanese were viciously beaten, and even issued with passbooks to prevent them seeking work elsewhere. Bound by their own culture to respect and do right by their new country and new employers, they kept their heads down and went about trying to duplicate Japanese village life on the plantations. But, like the Chinese before them, they left the plantations as soon as they could. Unlike the Chinese, they held on to the belief that they would one day return home to their villages. Many did leave but not for home. They went to the American mainland, where they were exposed to other ideas and influences. The Japanese Government, like the Chinese empire before it – and not before time – finally chose to restrict the emigration of its own people to the plantations.

Only slightly deterred, the Haoles then decided that it would be easier to deal with their own, American, officials and started to import a labour-force from one of their own colonies, the Philippines.

Meanwhile the Chinese had become competitive and successful merchants. The Japanese started to do the same. Their sons did not. They seized on education and went into white-collar jobs. Their life-style became better than it would have been at home, so they stayed and worked their way upwards through education and organization.

When Congress finally forced universal suffrage on the island in 1852, the whites did everything within their power to hold on to and manipulate political control. Determined not to be taken over by a 'yellow peril' and even more determined not to allow the orientals to participate in the political processes, they pulled the native Hawaiians, including the King, into alliances with them via bribery, corruption and promises. In a new constitution the Haoles were allowed to retain their foreign citizenship while Japanese and Chinese were not allowed to vote. At the same time, they kept the orientals – who were now Americans – out of any influential jobs. They restricted their language schools and censored their newspapers. They threatened and intimidated. But the new American Japanese were more outspoken, more articulate and more determined to take full advantage of American 'democracy'.

Then came Pearl Harbor. The racism already endemic in Hawaii intensified. Deportation was proposed, and internment. Deportation was turned down not so much for humanitarian reasons but because the problem of shipping almost forty per cent of the population to the mainland during wartime was insuperable. More than 100,000 were, however, put into internment camps. Many AJAs – Americans of Japanese Ancestry – were serving in the Hawaiian National Guard; another problem to be faced was what to do with them. The solution was to form another Hawaiian battalion and train them on the mainland. The AJAs fought in North Africa and in Europe. Later, volunteers served in Italy and France.

When these servicemen returned home to Hawaii, there was no way they would be content to let the old order continue. It didn't – and doesn't. Japanese Americans entered the political arena and rose to the top. They took the American system, twisted it around and beat the Americans at their own game. Today they are as unpopular as they ever were. Hawaii's senators are Japanese; the education department is run by Japanese; business and real estate are all in Japanese-American hands. And some of those hands reach back across the Pacific to less welcome ones, back in old Japan.

A headline in the *Honolulu Advertiser* had caught my eye: 'Yakuza Started Slowly Here, Then Came on Strong,' it said. The Yakuza are the Japanese Mafia, an organized-crime syndicate. They started their activities in Hawaii in a relatively small way in the early seventies, providing the services that businessmen the world over – and Japanese businessmen in particular – appear to need away from home: prostitution, pornography and gambling. Then some high-ups from one of the larger Tokyo-based gangs were involved in gun-running and drug-trafficking – not just the marijuana smuggling, for which Hawaii is famous, but cocaine too. There were brutal gangland killings. Connections were found to other crime syndicates, the most notorious being Hong Kong's Triads. But the Hawaiian Americans became most startled when the Japanese began to invest in Hawaiian real estate. Then a Japanese bank bought a California bank. This finally brought home the realization that not only was Hawaii being colonized but, possibly worse, the Japanese had taken over the market-place and were doing very nicely, thank you. So what price Pearl Harbor?

★

In a state that has fostered, encouraged and institutionalized racism and disharmony among both its indigenous and its immigrant peoples, it is not very difficult to realize where the original Hawaiians are in all this. The forces of social and economic domination have sent them hurtling to the bottom of the social heap.

Polynesians had been sailing the Pacific for hundreds of years, migrating from Indonesia northwards to Palau and the Carolines or taking a southern route through the Samoas and the Gilbert and Ellice islands. They were extraordinary journeys made by extraordinary sailors. Carrying their food, animals and plants with them, and navigating by the stars and wave patterns, they reached almost all the islands of the Pacific between Malaya and Peru, New Zealand and Hawaii. No one knows when the first settlers came to Hawaii, but it is known they were from the Marquesas, now part of French Polynesia. They were succeeded by Polynesians from Tahiti itself and Bora-Bora. By the time Cook arrived in 1779, there was a complex and sophisticated social system already in place.

The islands were divided into a series of small kingdoms, usually at war with each other. The Hawaiians knew how to sail, how to navigate, how to fish and how to grow food. They were experienced craftsmen in wood and stone. Theirs was a highly stratified society, with para-mount chiefs and lesser chiefs as the top layer, priests and skilled craftsmen next. Lower down the social scale came the ordinary citizens. At the very bottom of the heap were the kauwa, the outcasts or slaves. The structure was kept together by the religious system called Kapu – taboo as it later became known. The priests regulated behaviour according to Kapu, and were ruthless with anyone stepping out of line. Corporal and capital punishment were common.

When the *Discovery* arrived at Kealakekua Bay on what is today called the Big Island, the expedition was on its way to try to find land between New Zealand and Cape Horn. It landed at the island to trade nails for food. The Polynesians thought Cook to be a reincarnation of one of their gods, and the King gave the expedition a lavish welcome as one would a returning god. But the entertaining of gods is expensive, and Cook's sailors had insatiable appetites for food and women. It was no doubt with a sigh of relief that the natives watched the expedition sail off again into the sunset. But bad weather damaged one of *Discovery's* masts and the expedition was forced to return to the island.

Avid for nails and any other bits of higher technology they could lay their hands on, the Hawaiians eventually stole the *Discovery's* cutter. Planning to hold the King hostage in return for the cutter, Cook and a group of sailors went ashore. When they landed, the natives started throwing stones. The sailors remaining aboard *Discovery* opened fire. As Cook turned to shout orders to stop the firing, he stumbled. Somebody stabbed him from behind. Then, perhaps seeing his mortality, the crowd fell on him and it was all over.

A year after Cook's death the old Polynesian King also died, and his nephew, Kamehameha, decided to settle some old scores. He built a fleet of war-canoes and set out to conquer the other islands, including Oahu, which he did. Under Kamehameha's leadership the Hawaiian islands were united. It was the beginning of the Hawaiian monarchy and the end of the social and taboo systems of the old Polynesian culture and society.

There were nearly a dozen Hawaiian monarchs on the throne before American planters overthrew the Queen and the Government and in 1893 the islands were annexed. In just over a hundred years, members of the Hawaiian royal family had travelled all over Europe and America and did

Waikiki Beach at Honolulu, the state capital of Hawaii.

Public telephones on Waikiki Beach.

An offering being made to Pele, the goddess of the volcano, at Kilauea Crater on Hawaii, the Big Island.

A white shutterboard church on Hawaii, the Big Island; one of the many
shipped out by American missionaries.

all the things that visiting royal families have always done: they wined, dined, admired the Crown Jewels in the Tower of London and went to the theatre. Some Kings leaned towards Britain, others towards the United States. One of the young princes, who had travelled to Europe to learn something of the Haoles' land, died of measles while visiting the Court of St James. King Kalakaua had a coronation ceremony that borrowed much from Napoleon and not a little from Gilbert and Sullivan. Kamehameha III, built the Iolani Palace along European lines, holding grand balls and dressing ministers and officials in vaguely Ruritanian uniforms.

The Sandwich Islands, as they were then called, had become part of the expanding commercial network of the United States' Pacific coast. The economy had long been in the hands of the American fur-traders and whaling companies, and the completion of the Panama Canal invited further expansion. One of the reviews of the day wrote:

> The growth of our own Pacific States, the development of the Canadian coast, the project of completion of the Panama Canal . . . the progress of Chile as a naval and commercial power, the immense expansion of Australian population and interests; the modernization of Japan and the awakening commercial life of China . . . all these things point to a colossal future trade for the Pacific.

The islands were seen as the key to the North Pacific.

It was a woman, Queen Liliuokalani, who decided that it was time to restore the royal power that her predecessor King Kalakaua, had signed away to the Haoles even before annexation.[1] Liliuokalani's attempt to bring in a new constitution and restore a little more power to the monarchy was too much for the planter oligarchy. The white businessmen dominated the new economy, and they were not going to sign over their power to a bunch of indigenous Hawaiians. In favour of annexing the islands to the

USA, they formed the euphemistically named 'Committee of Public Safety'. They had already created a militia and a Provisional Government; now they took the precaution of calling in the marines to help them take over the Government. The American President, Cleveland, actually refused to annex the islands at this stage but the self-styled Provisional Government refused to step down and coolly established a republic under the pineapple king Sandford Dole, whose factory today is one of the great tourist attractions of the island. Four years later, in 1898, under US President McKinley, Hawaii was formally annexed and Dole abdicated from the 'presidency' to become Territorial Governor. Today, the street and hotel names are all that remain to remind you that there was ever a Hawaiian monarchy at all: Kalakaua Avenue, Kamehameha Highway, the Prince Kuhio Hotel.

At the end of Milan Kundera's *The Book of Laughter and Forgetting*, the author is interviewed by Philip Roth. Kundera talks of what happens when a big power deprives a small country of its national consciousness; of the proscribing and eradication of literature, architecture, history. 'A nation which loses awareness of its past gradually loses its self,' he says at one point. Liliuokalani's palace was now America's own, and native Hawaiians were reduced to entertaining tourists in some electronic, light-entertainment form of hula, the original having been banned by the missionaries. It took the Russians no time and the invasion of 1968 to reduce Czechoslovakia's sense of self. In Hawaii it took the Americans longer – seventy-five years.

★

Honolulu and Waikiki were getting me down. I was tired of the junk souvenirs, the tat, the food, the crowds and the overriding dedication to shopping and eating.

In small, tree-lined alleys off Kalakaua Avenue, Chinese and Filipino women ran stalls of cheap beads and plastic wind-up dolls that hulaed. The original frangipani leis –

garlands of sweet-smelling and welcoming flowers handed to visitors and travellers – had been replaced by leis made up of plastic flowers, candies, even miniature whisky bottles. Murderous-looking oysters lurked in bowls of murky water for passers-by to pry open in the hope of finding a pearl. It was all a hideous combination of the Costa Brava and Hong Kong, an assault to eyes and ears. Where there wasn't junk to buy there was junk to eat – yakitori shish kebab, next to Heidi's German ice-cream parlour, refried beans, tacos and noodles. In a multi-storey car-park attached to a shopping centre, a group of old Japanese men sat eating noodles out of take-away cardboard boxes while carbon-monoxide fumes filled the air.

At night, another kind of market took over. Thai and Filipino girls and boys hung around on street corners. Cruising cars filled with the bloom of American youth hooted and yelled and catcalled. I watched a man slowly kerb-crawl a boy no more than fourteen years old, waiting while the boy went into a supermarket, kerb-crawling him again when he came out. It was reminiscent of all too many places – Sunset Strip, Bangkok – so I rented a car and drove the length of Oahu to see Waimea Falls.

The Falls are in a forest reserve, and I hoped to lose the crowds and walk through the rain-forest. But it was Sunday, and once I left the freeway it was bumper-to-bumper queueing. Anything unorganized was out of the question. Toytown buses and open trams were on hand to take the tourists to wherever they wanted to go. Under the trees, Asian wedding-groups – mostly Korean – were having home-videos taken of brides, grooms and wedding-guests. The forest was neatly landscaped, with little paths that wound away from and then met up again with the tarmac and the Toytown tram. It was Disneyland and *Alice in Wonderland* all in one. As I queued again to get out of the forest, I realized that the entire island of Oahu was a giant playground from which you couldn't escape.

The centre of the island – that gloriously tempting chain of mountains and the surrounding tropical forest –

was impossible to penetrate because it is one big military reserve. Twenty-five per cent of Oahu is a military installation of one kind or another, and the small island of Kaho'olawe, just south of Maui, has for years been used for bombing practice by the US navy. During the Rim of the Pacific, or RIMPAC, exercises it takes an even further battering when the assembled navies of five nations bomb it from the sea and air. For the Hawaiians this is a total assault upon the island, the earth and many of their religious beliefs. There are some precious archeological sites on the island, but excavation would be impossible because of the numbers of unexploded shells and bombs.

Since the Second World War, Hawaii has been one of the main US Marines centres for guerrilla training, naval manoeuvres and mock nuclear-submarine warfare; for experimental defoliation and rehearsal runs of tactical bombing. The Korean, Laotian and Vietnamese wars were all masterminded from Hawaii, and Camp Smith on Oahu is the headquarters of the US Pacific Command – USPACOM, as it likes to be called – responsible for the security of ten million square miles of the Pacific and Indian Oceans and some 380,000 military personnel. Only a hundred miles away, little Maui is a nuclear-free zone!

★

Henrietta and William Vitorelli had lived for years in Micronesia, the American Pacific, in Palau and Guam. They were Quakers and were now in their eighties. Now they lived on Maui. Henrietta was firm on the phone: 'Stay on the north coast, near the airport – it's cheaper and easier to get to us. Look out for a dirt road; it's the one with all the mailboxes, yellow mailboxes. See you Sunday 2.30, after lunch.'

Maui has white sand beaches and two volcanoes, at opposite ends of the island. There are rolling valleys between. The light changes continually over the mountains; menacing cloud banks build up and there are sudden, quick thunderstorms. On the south shore, Lahaina used to be a second centre of the whaling trade, along with Honolulu, with sometimes as many as five hundred ships moored offshore. Today the town has been restored to a tourist showpiece, sanitized into a clean, quaint and totally pretentious historical postcard that has nothing to do with how it was when the crews of the whalers stopped off for rest and recreation. But, despite the cleaning-up and the tourists, Maui's history feels very near to the surface. There are still rich, fertile valleys of sugar-cane with narrow railway-lines running alongside. The old sugar-refineries disgorge a combination of unpalatable-looking black smoke and a pleasant, sticky, molasses smell at the same time. In the foothills of the mountains stretch the pineapple plantations, the slightly blue-tinged tops of the pineapple plants surfacing above the deep-red earth. Like the other Hawaiian islands, Maui has a profusion of New England churches. When the missionaries arrived here in the 1820s they at first shipped their churches out wholesale, so throughout the islands, behind hedges of crotons and under the shade of flame-trees, sit these remnants of New England, white or green clapboard with red barn roofs and spindly steeples.

Travelling east to Henrietta and Vit's, I drove through neat, winding country lanes bordered by English-sized fields. Cattle and horses lazily flicked away the flies and the heat. Pomegranates hung in the hedgerows instead of blackberries. It was a Sunday afternoon and had the feel of Sunday afternoons everywhere. Henrietta's directions were perfect. I saw the yellow mailboxes before the turn-off. At the end of the dirt track lined with vegetable plots there were two houses: one large, one small. The small one was low and made of timber and coral. Orchids clung on to a tree trunk which grew up through the centre of the small patio. The tree's branches shaded the small house. I slid open the fly-screen door but I was early; there was nobody in except cats. Across the lawn was a herb garden with row after row of basil bushes, sage, and lemon balm.

A chicken-run had been built under banana palms which dripped with flowers and clusters of bananas. The whole lot sat on the top of a cliff looking out to the deep blue of the Pacific. The trade winds blew the strong, rich smell of the basil back towards the house. It seemed a good place to have retired to.

The Vitorellis must have been a stunning-looking couple when they were younger. Tall and big-boned and both dressed in white, they still were.

Vit said he had been in Micronesia for about twenty-four years altogether. He had gone there originally with the navy, in 1949.

'The impact of the US Administration hadn't hit the islands then,' he said. 'The devastation and the misery of war had. Up in the rural areas they still had the traditional religion very much in place. The Japanese persecuted and tortured people trying to get rid of that religion, but they didn't succeed. The more they tried the more deeply, they got entrenched. I've seen some of the old, old people without hands, feet chopped off during the Japanese war period,' he said. 'You know, the early periods in Palau are not really understood by Americans.'

After the war, Vit had been working as a district administrator, setting up schools and working in community development. He advocated self-sufficiency for the native Palauans, and in 1954, at the height of the McCarthy period, the American Administration tried to get rid of him as a security risk. His case was taken to the Supreme Court and he was exonerated and reinstated.

'I had an awful hard time,' Vit said. 'Whenever the Republican Administration got in I was relegated to a desk and a typewriter.'

What did he think was going on at the time?

'Subversion – actual conscious conspiracy,' he said firmly. 'Subversion of the people in order to get their land. They took away their identity; they took away their land. They did it many times. They did it in order to make them subservient and dependent. I never used to believe that

until a lot of the facts came out. It was the Americaniza-
tion of Palau – establishing a dependency, with handouts
rather than earnings.'

'What about the Palauans' identification with other
Polynesian groups and Pacific nations?' I asked.

'Non-existent,' said Vit firmly. 'The Gaumanians and
the Palauans or the Trukese, each one feels they're
superior. They were surprised when they found people
from other groups felt the same way.'

'This transmigration of people – in search of education,
work, the offer of US citizenship and all that goes with it –
what are you going to have left in these island societies?'
I asked him.

'Nothing,' said Vit. 'You're going to have a composite.
It's already happened on Guam. It's happening in Tahiti.
Saipan is going fast. Here it's pretty well gone. You don't
have any Hawaiian culture here. You have Hawaiian
groups trying to recapture themselves, but this can't be
done; they can't do it, no matter how they try. They can
never be Hawaiian again.'

He shook his head sadly. 'If you know the Hawaiians,
you feel the hatred. Most of the jails are full of Hawaiians,
more than any other ethnic group. They don't have the
shrewdness of knowing how to cope and finagle which you
have to in America. They get jobs, but they're menial
jobs. There's no good feelings between Hawaiians and
American business. You have to know how to pull off a
deal, but they're not that kind. Theirs is a sharing society.
The land thing – that's the worst. They've just been
screwed. These young people – they have no land, they
have no jobs, they're lost. Now they're trying to get their
land back. It's a lost cause, but they're still trying. They
have a small nationalistic group. It makes some headway,
but not enough to count.'

Henrietta sat quietly on the grass between us. For
a moment Vit was sad and thoughtful. For a moment he
looked his age.

'You may not want to hear this,' he said nervously, 'but

I think . . . well, the island people – Oceania,' he said – 'all these island people are going to be subservient to the Japanese domination of the Pacific. The United States and Europe are going to be a big balance of power against China, Japan, Indonesia, Australia . . . a new balance of power. It's happening already.'

I didn't disagree with him.

★

Driving back through a golden evening light that presaged a tropical thunderstorm, I wondered just how serious the issue of Hawaiian nationalism was. It wasn't the first time I'd heard about Hawaiians' growing anger, although I doubted their ability to get their lands back from the American military.

Under American law there are two kinds of Hawaiian: native Hawaiians and Hawaiians. Native Hawaiians have fifty per cent or more indigenous Hawaiian blood in their veins; other Hawaiians have less.

The Hawaiian land and sovereignty issue was inordinately complicated, not least because several of the Hawaiian groups oppose each other over the details.

When America annexed the islands, Queen Lilikuolani was on the throne. At the time of the overthrow, she ceded more than a million acres to the US Government. Fifty years later, when Hawaii became a state, the federal Government returned the majority of the ceded lands to the new state with the mandate to manage them as a public trust. Some of this land was handed back to be used as homelands for native Hawaiians, some was to be held in public trust both for native Hawaiians and for the general public. Some, however, still remains firmly with the federal Government of the USA. This includes the airport, public parks and harbours. Just to complicate matters, there is also land that has been retained for use by the federal Government, administered by the various state departments, such as Transport and Natural Resources. Under a constitutional amendment, twenty per cent of all funds from the 'public land trust' is to go to the Office of Hawaiian Affairs for the education and 'betterment of conditions of native Hawaiians'. It is the unreceived revenues from these lands that the Hawaiians and the Office of Hawaiian Affairs feel entitled to but are not getting. That's not the whole story, but it nearly is.

Two names dominate the Hawaiian sovereignty movement: sisters, Haunani Kay Trask and Milinani Trask. It was hard to find any Hawaiian to talk about the issues at all. One Saturday I took the bus westwards for more than two hours along Oahu's dismal south shore to rendezvous with an activist in the parking-lot of the local Burger King. The drive became increasingly depressing – the houses poorer, the beaches and seashore more unkempt the further away from Honolulu I got. This was not tourist country, and no efforts had been made to clean up the litter or the beaches. The activist never arrived, and the contact number was out of order. I sat in the parking-lot of the Burger King and watched the local families who had come to shop at the local five-and-dime, before taking the dreary drive back.

On the Monday I arranged to meet somebody at the Office of Hawaiian Affairs who would tell me about the land-rights issue. She didn't arrive either. I failed to track down Haunani Kay Trask at the university, so I heaved a sigh of relief when her sister, Milinani, finally agreed to see me.

An attorney, Milinani Trask was not only a native Hawaiian but also the Governor of the self-styled Lahui Hawaii – Nation of Hawaii. A strikingly beautiful young woman with a strong face, dark eyes and a thick black plait hanging down her back, she looked like a true descendant of the goddess Pele, the Queen of Fire. Milinani too was very fiery.

'You must understand, the situation in Hawaii is unique in the United States of America,' she said. 'When the legal government was overthrown – that was Queen Lilikuolani – it was forced to cede its land. That's C.E.D.E.,' she pointed at my notebook. I kept my mouth shut.

'If you cede,' she continued, 'the sovereign that accepts the act of cession must promise to protect the people and their property rights. When Hawaii came into the union, twenty-five per cent of lands were given to the state to hold in trust for two classes of people: the public and the native. The state's interpretation of that was that natives are part of the public so we're not going to do a damn thing for natives: we'll take all of the trust money and use it for other purposes.'

She lit a cigarette. 'The second thing was that, until 1961, the federal policy relating to native American people – Indians, Eskimos, Innouits and others – was one of termination.' She saw the expression on my face. 'When you study native-American legal history, there is a period from 1940 to 1961 called the "termination" era. During that time the federal Government, through the Bureau of Indian Affairs, identified certain native peoples who they wanted to terminate out of existence. . . . Certain native-American tribes were singled out to be exterminated legally.'*

'Wait a minute, are you saying . . .?'

She ignored me and carried on. 'Because we came to statehood at this time, Hawaiians and all of their land-holdings were turned over to the state to manage it in trust for the native people. Because the native people are wards of the state and the federal Government acts as their legal grandparent, the native people are not allowed to go into the federal district court to bring an action to protect their own trust land.' She leaned across the desk. 'We're the only native Americans remaining in this country, and we're the only remaining racial classification of American citizens who are not allowed to go into the federal court to challenge the state's breach of our trust lands. There is so much evidence of complicity, of illegally utilizing native trust lands; there is every indication, well-documented, that the federal government and the state law acted in concert to withhold land from the native people.'

She stopped to light another cigarette while I drew a deep breath and tried to gather my thoughts and the implications of what she was saying.

'The bulk of the Hawaiian homelands are used by the state – federal and county agencies. Thousands of acres are leased out to non-Hawaiians, primarily Japanese,' she said accusingly – 'Japanese who are in the legislature; Japanese who are friends of Dan Inouye.' Dan Inouye was the state Senator, a Japanese American. 'Now if you look at who the non-Hawaiians are who have benefited from these lands illegally, by and large they're all Japanese – local – connected to the Democratic party.

'In 1978 we went into the legislature. We said, "Look, the state is not managing our lands. What we would like is a native corporation to transfer our lands to us." The state responds by creating OHA – the Office of Hawaii Affairs, patterned after the Bureau of Indian Affairs. They say because we have OHA, created by the state, we're not entitled to have a nation. What we are saying is that it's time to extend this and to have a native-Hawaiian nation. Indian self-determination, Indian civil-rights acts get passed; Hawaiians don't get included in any of those things. What we are saying is, if America's other native people are entitled to have self-governing mechanisms, we are entitled to the same.'

She tapped an angry finger on the desk. 'The Indian nations do not pay taxes on their land. Why are Hawaiian homesteaders made to pay taxes on their land? Our lands should be tax-exempt. The Indians raise funds by taxing people who do business on their land. If you're Chevron and you want to pump gas, you go to Indian land and not only do you not have to pay federal and state taxes but you

---

* Trask was confusing 'terminate' and 'exterminate' here. It is true that, during the Eisenhower years of the fifties, the policy was to make everyone an American. Legally, many people were no longer considered Indian – but double standards existed according to what tribe you were from and what percentage of Indian blood you had.

have to pay Indian taxes which are always a cent or two cheaper. So the Indian nations are given the opportunity to raise capital with a taxing mechanism, and that is one of the incidences of sovereignty.

'OHA gets state revenues of about $1.5 million a year. They have $5 million in the bank right now. They utilize seventy-five per cent of their revenues to pay their own salaries,' she said scornfully, lighting another cigarette.

'There is not a greater human tragedy in this country among native people than with native Hawaiians. I agree that the Indians have gotten the shaft, and just because they have 307 nations it doesn't mean that they're all doing good, but at least they have the foundation on which to build something for their people. We are denied even that.'

She spoke in short, staccato bursts – a kind of angry shorthand. I was impressed by her and I liked her, but her vehemence frightened me.

'A lot of things have happened in this struggle. There's been people killed. They will not stop with murder, you know. I got a bunch of calls saying "you'd better knock it off – don't challenge the state's holding – we're gonna get your family." My family no longer lives on this island, only my sister Hananiki and I. Because we are leaders in the Hawaiian community and we have to fight them, we stay here; but my mother, my brothers, their families, my sisters all live on the Big Island.

'It's millions, it's billions of dollars. What is behind geothermal development?' she answered her own question. 'Geothermal water, deep-ocean leasing, manganese-nodule mining – all of these things are assets of the native trusts. So we don't just have a claim for half the public lands but all the appurtenances thereto appertaining – that's legal language – and that means . . .' – she paused for breath – 'natural resources. Why has Dan Inouye been pushing a $750 billion project to develop geothermal and to bring it to Maui and to bring it to Oahu? The reason? When you look at the state plans, it services the energy needs of Waikiki and Lahaina. Eighty-four per cent of the hotels on Waikiki are owned by Japanese foreign investors, one is owned by United States business and the rest are divided by other foreign business.

'You know, of course, America is a debtor nation to Japan. We're a Japanese colony, and the funny thing is that we've been made that way by Japanese governors. Look at our representatives in Senate and Congress – they're Japanese. The question of war reparations has been floating round for ten years. They got *their* reparations. Hawaiian reparations went to Congress in 1967. We haven't seen a single cent.'

Then, too, there was the definition of a Hawaiian. This was to be changed so that it would no longer be necessary to have fifty per cent indigenous Hawaiian blood to be classed as a native Hawaiian. 'They're gonna make it any blood quantum,' said Milinani, outraged. 'Why do they want to have a change in the definition of native Hawaiian? They want to change the definition to say that "native Hawaiian" means a person who has any blood quantum of the blood of the people who were here prior to Cooks' landing, so it goes down to one ten-thousandth. And how do they prove it? By an affidavit when you go to register to vote.

'We will fight,' said Milinani, looking even more like her volcanic counterpart. 'For many years we have been proud to say that we are the only native people in America who have never resorted to violence. Now the writing is on the wall. What we are proposing is not revolutionary, it is not violent – it is in fact as American as apple-pie. If it wasn't, you wouldn't have 309 nations in this country with 308 being Indian nations.

'Now we've all kinds of modern problems. There's a lot of drug abuse. There's a lot of violence. Although we're twenty per cent of the population, we're eighty per cent of the incarcerated juvenile and adult population – and for crimes of violence, very high. We still have a lot of Vietnam vets dying from Agent-Orange poisoning, which was tested here in Hawaii. Last year, for the first time in the history of our modern struggle, we had native Hawaiians who took up the gun.'

She counted on her fingers. 'Drugs, alcohol, political frustration – too much time has passed and we've been peaceful. The patience of the people is wearing very thin,' she said wearily. 'Hawaiians,' she said – 'they take out the garbage, they wash the white man's laundry, and over generations you have a hell of a lot of hatred and animosity built up. Hawaii is far from being the melting-pot of the Pacific. You know, in Hawaii we have something called Kill Haole on Friday day – you wait for Friday to come along and you pick somebody who's white in your class and you beat the shit out of him. The last day of every school year, parents are driving to pick up their kids at two o'clock and waiting in the parking-lot because they don't want their kid to fall victim to Kill Haole on Friday day.

'Why are Canadian tourists beaten to death, shot? Why do we have these problems? It's not because there is a political terrorist group or political thought behind it. It's random violence. You know somebody treats you bad; you're sick of it – go out and look for the nearest person with white skin.

'On this island you cannot go to the beaches once the sun sets, 'cause when the sun sets those beach areas belong to the native people and if they catch anybody out there you're dead. I don't camp on beaches on this island any more at night, because they're at a point where they're not even checking you out. They see a tent, they figure, "Well, let's go", and discharge a clip of .45 shells in there or club the people to death. And, I mean, it could be me in the tent. You know, it could be me.'

Just for a moment she softened. 'The man who beats his wife when he's drugged up – he does not do it with impunity, he feels guilt and despair.'

I wished I could agree with her. I couldn't remember when I had last encountered so much anger. I wandered out of the tall glass building into downtown Honolulu, then I remembered: the goddess Pele was both creator and destroyer of new lands.

That weekend there was a conference on native Hawaiian rights up at the Kamehameha School, high in the hills above Honolulu. Milinani and her sister were both to take part. Perhaps the long afternoon spent with her had dulled me to less articulate proponents of the Hawaiian cause; perhaps I simply wasn't in the mood. One of the speakers equated himself to the Palestinians. 'We who are resistors,' he said, 'with no country to call our own, must reach out as an example.' I thought of the times I had spent in the camps of Sabra and Chatila in Beirut, and in villages on the West Bank. My patience threshold dropped to zero and I left.

★

According to Hawaiian mythology, Pele, the goddess of the volcano, was also the maker of mountains, the eater of land and the destroyer of forests. Today she is said to live on the Big Island of Hawaii. Legend says she went there after trying to make her home on each of the Hawaiian islands in turn, being chased from each by her elder sister, the goddess of the sea. Finally she made her home among the mountains of Hawaii.

I had never seen a volcano close to, and Hawaii has two active though, according to the experts, relatively gentle volcanoes: Mount Kilauea and Mauna Loa. Mount Kilauea has been erupting since 1983 – not a spectacular eruption, with flames bursting from the top of the crater, but a network of lava tubes winding their way through the side of the mountain to hit the sea with a hiss of steam and heat eight miles further on. This means that the island is growing daily, because of the amounts of new land added to the shoreline.

I liked the idea of the bigness of the island. Maui was pretty, but too contained. The other islands were even smaller. Perhaps on the Big Island it might be possible to lose the incessant chatter of tourists.

After Honolulu, Hilo had the right feel to it. It was the right scale, and conjured up images of Herman Melville and James Michener. There was a small fish market, and weatherbeaten wooden buildings flopped lopsidedly against each other. San Francisco and Honolulu must have looked like this once upon a time. After the purple orchids and overkill of Oahu, it was restful to the eyes. At the end of a rainy afternoon, I strolled down Banyan Drive, the trees' great tendrils flopping lugubriously down huge trunks on to the grass below.

I planned to circuit the island, starting with Mount Kilauea, on through the national park with its chain of craters, then along the southern shore to Kealakekua Bay where Captain Cook had been killed. The return route would be back across the highest peak in the Pacific, Mauna Kea, to Hilo. It was entirely fanciful, because I had absolutely no idea of how big the Big Island really was and I was short of time.

Setting off before dawn, a gentle rain sloughed off the mountains. Hilo was surrounded with lush tropical under-growth that soon gave way to forests. The forests gave way to light woodland, and the woodland to a kind of heathland with ferns and lichens and small twisted trees. There was no sense of altitude, and the road stretched black and wet straight ahead. Nearly three hours later I was at the entrance of the national park, where I picked up a map and set off for the craters. The sun broke through the early-morning mist and there was just a touch of warmth.

It was like being on the top of moorland on a misty morning, except that the mist wasn't mist at all but puffs of steam like gas jets pumping out of the earth. The ground puffed and blew and steamed. There was no noise, just a rhythmical puffing and pumping like an old, slow steam engine. It was eerily quiet. Small ferns and twisted trunks of small trees grew out of a kind of golden and grey tundra; there was no green.

The Rock Islands of Palau. There are 200 of these islands, all uninhabited.

A gathering of matais and Talking Chiefs in a ceremonial fale on Western Samoa. The fale is raised from the ground on volcanic lava.

Talking Chiefs make speeches at the funeral of a matai. Samoans pride themselves on their gifts of oratory.

A traditional fale in Western Samoa. These houses have no walls, but woven blinds can be let down for privacy or as protection against the weather.

Two Western Samoan boys inside a fale.

Piula Methodist church, Western Samoa. The church stands in a well-known beauty spot above a natural freshwater pool fed by a spring.

Robert Louis Stevenson's tomb on Mount Vaea, above Apia, Western Samoa.

An aerial view of Pago Pago, in American Samoa.

I walked to the edge of what I called the crater but volcanologists call the caldera. I don't know what I had expected, but it wasn't this – a vast, deep and dead-looking giant saucer. It stretched for miles, flat black and brown – a gigantic cow-pat. Its size and flatness was awe-inspiring. On one side of the caldera a sulphurous yellow gas steamed. I wondered what was going on underneath it all. Strangest of all was the quiet: it was as though I had landed on the moon or the top of the world. Behind me the broad steaming plain; in front, a deadly gaping crater so wide you could hardly see across to the other side.

The guidebooks and maps describe Kilauea's eruptions as 'mild'. There were even paths across the crater for hikers. I ventured down into the crater. Standing on the outside, the sun had been shining and I felt I was still somewhere on the earth, albeit on the edge. Suddenly, deep down inside the caldera, it all changed. Black clouds arranged themselves overhead and Pele's tears rained down. As I wandered along a track, great fissures of uprooted lava and pumice made ridges and canyons that plunged several yards deep. Sometimes the overall blackness of the volcano crust gave way to a burnt copper colour. The rain pelted down, and steam hung over the crater. The strong, sour smell of sulphur rose. Mount Kilauea looked and felt like hell on earth. I ran out of the rain and back to the car, deciding that the older craters might prove more manageable.

At the side of the road, an occasional charcoaled tree burst forth out of the black dried-up mass which looked like dried tar. The Hawaiians call this shiny, black, satin-like lava 'pahoehoe'. As it cools, the lava folds and creases, taking on wrinkles and lines and looking like a cross between tar and oil.

On the downward climb towards the sea, the eroded hills and savannah gave way to tropical rain-forest again, and stunted grey wiliwilis were replaced by tall tree-ferns. The volcanoes' presence was everywhere. Over the years, the eruptions had forced the lava straight down to the sea, destroying forest, agricultural land and fishing villages. Great black turds of lava, some more than a mile wide, looked as though they had been thrust up from the centre of the earth. It was as though God, in a rage, had punched his fist up through the earth's crust. Appropriately, I passed a sign advertising the Church of the Messianic Word. Then the smell of dank forest and steam gave way to eucalyptus and frangipani, a hedge of bougainvillaea and an orchard of macadamia trees. Out of nothingness, I came to simple wooden bungalows and fishing villages, and the sun shone again, although the beaches were black.

I never made it to Kealakekua Bay, because somewhere on the way I passed a white painted sign pointing down a narrow lane, saying simply, 'Painted Church'. A lane wound along the top of the cliff with a drop to the ocean on one side. Tucked between almost suburban villas and gardens was a small white and green wooden church with a latticed porch and a kind of ridiculous inverted leg-of-mutton frill at the base of its spire. It reminded me of Romania or northern Europe. Inside, the pillars were wreathed in bright blues and reds – ribbons, butterflies and flowers. Great painted green leaves crept up and over the ceiling. It was breathtakingly pretty, but outside sat two Hawaiian ladies with flowers in their hair, touting for tourist trade.

It was to this southern coast – the Kona coast – that many of the Japanese farmers came when they fled the plantations. They planted coffee, mostly for white land-owners; hence kona coffee and, presumably, Cona coffee machines. Today the largest land-owners are the Portuguese, descendents of those ranchers who were recruited for the plantations in the last quarter of the nineteenth century. Originally from Madeira and the Azores, now they own great ranches on the centre of the island and breed beef for export to the mainland.

Inland, the road turned away from the sea and across another great plain of lava. A kind of tufted pampas grass in the palest gold grew through the black pumice. In the afternoon light the grass turned white and silver. The road was a single narrow band cutting through the tundra for as far as I could see. It was as I had always imagined Patagonia to be, or parts of Alaska. After thirty-five miles of sameness, a truck passed me coming from the opposite direction. At last the road was broken by a crossroads leading to a small town.

Clouds hung over the tiny clapboard church, sitting alone in a green meadow, and fat black cows grazed under casuarinas and eucalyptus. Nasturtiums tumbled wild alongside the road, reminding me of an English summer, and kids rode by on fat, shiny ponies. After the Plain of Jars, a Dorset lane with Thelwell ponies and busy Lizzies. I had to choose between Dorset or up and over the dirt road of another volcano, Mauna Kea. I decided on the soft option. After the wooded lanes, a great blue ribbon broke out on my left, the clouds stopped abruptly, and the ribbon merged with the sky. The ribbon was the Pacific, looking as it should – dancing white with foam. Then, not like Dorset at all, cane-fields unfolded down as far as the edge of the sea, golden in the late evening light. If Cook had lost his cutter on this gentler shore, maybe the subsequent events would have been different.

From the slopes of Mauna Kea, rushing silver streams ran into the sea, each more spectacular than the last. They dropped over shiny, black volcanic rocks deep in palm-crowded gulleys. It was all lushness and light, a land of milk and honey.

Outside Hilo, I stopped at an Asian cemetery – Japanese or Korean – peaceful and Pacific. At the foot of the headstones, families had left offerings of oranges and flowers and bottles of beer. Wind-chimes blew softly. I realized that I hadn't seen a single piece of molten lava, let alone a flame, but it didn't matter much.

★

I had come to Hawaii to see Martin Wolff, a lawyer who fled to Honolulu from Palau after his house was fire-bombed. A long story, it had to do with the assassination of the then President of Palau, Haruo Remelik. Palau was a former trust territory of the United States. In a way it still is. The Palau story is a complex one and ongoing; it involves assassination, murder, trial without jury, wrongful arrest and a British company. All, it would appear, with the connivance and encouragement of people in Washington and Hawaii – people who are not far removed from the Washington Administration.

Wolff lived in Waikiki and had a reputation for being something of a self-publicist. There was hardly a day when a story about him didn't feature in the local paper. A born-again Christian, he was part of the Jimmy Swaggart ministry, and spottable from a mile off. When I went to see him, he was standing on the balcony of his apartment block with a portable phone clamped to his ear. He waved cheerfully.

All the people I had spoken to about the Palau murders had referred to Wolff. Although they didn't all take him seriously, they all liked him. It was easy to see why. Small and dapper, he was charming. He had the smallest feet I had seen on anyone.

'Would you prefer to keep the door open?' he asked when I went into the apartment, worried for my sensitivities at being alone with him.

We talked of this and that and Hawaii and Palau.

'Look,' he said later, over dinner. 'In forty years the Japanese built 56 miles of road. They built fountains. There were no cars, just bikes. The US destroyed the roads yet every Palauan ended up owning a car. There are just seven miles of paved road. The schools are still using textbooks from the Kennedy Administration. The Peace Corps gave them marijuana and herpes. We gave them Budweiser, blue jeans and Marlborough.

'The trust territory had traditionally been a dumping ground for drugs, drink and derelicts,' he continued, 'and the problem with the Palauans was that they were politically astute – they picked up all the wrong things at the right time.' He laughed. 'The only reason Salii got elected,' said Wolff, 'was that he bought the electorate.' Salii was the successor to the assassinated President. 'You know,' he said, 'he paid the taxi drivers twenty dollars for every person they brought to the poll.'

Like Bill Vitorelli, Wolff agonized over the lack of tradition left to the islanders. The new systems of money and power were in conflict with tribal power as it had once existed, and the advent of the welfare package had merely served to advance the decay. He struck a chill when he said, 'We created the environment. We created the man. Palau is the next Philippines. We don't learn a thing. If Salii is re-elected and not assassinated, we will have our next Marcos.'

I did not realize at the time how right he would prove to be.

Chapter 4

PALAU

TROUBLES IN PARADISE

I t was months earlier, in London, that I had first heard of the Palau story. I had bumped into a former colleague, a producer with one of the American television networks. We had talked of my going back to the Pacific.

'You must do something on Palau,' he had said. 'It's a hell of a story – got everything: drugs, murder, arson, a presidential assassination. It was too big for us to handle, but in a book you've got the space.'

The following day, a motor-cycle messenger arrived with envelopes full of files, company searches and copies of telexes.

Reading through the files, I got the slightly uneasy feeling I was eavesdropping on some major skulduggery that I shouldn't know about and certainly didn't quite understand, a scandal that was in the process of being investigated but had not been resolved. There were hints of conspiracy, of big names in the US Administration being involved in pay-offs, bribes and murder. The top of a Pacific iceberg. The whole affair appeared to have started with the building of a power station and had ended with the assassination of the island's President. There was an awful lot of mayhem in between.

I hunted for the island in *The Times Atlas of the World* and eventually found it to the north of Papua New Guinea and east of something called the Philippine Trench, an archipelago of islands too small and too numerous for the atlas to give any clear idea of just how many there were or what their geography might be.

An unlikely name cropped up several times in the files, that of a former detective sergeant in the Kent Constabulary, Barrie Thompson. Thompson was apparently the only private eye in Britain investigating white-collar fraud. His involvement with the Palau story started on behalf of a client, a Palestinian financier living in Paris, who had lost $9 million investing in the British company that had built a power plant on Palau. The company, Ipseco, was operating in and around the Pacific and had recently been declared bankrupt. Thompson was out to try to get the Palestinian some of his money back.

When he first started his investigation, Thompson had little idea of the size of the Pacific and thought, like many before him, that it was made up of a series of tropical island paradises, each one more beautiful than the next, all of them a replica of Tahiti. Up until then he had never heard of Palau or Micronesia. He wasn't alone in that: the North Pacific has never conjured up the same kind of romanticism as the South Pacific, although some of the islands are just as beautiful. There are thousands of tiny islands, atolls and islets surrounded by iridescent lagoons and crystal waters, beaches fringed by palm trees and tropical jungles, although few of them have the mountainous beauty of Papua New Guinea or Tahiti. What they do have is wonderful marine life.

Some islands are so small and insignificant that they aren't really islands at all but atolls. The American writer Eugene Burdick said that an atoll 'is a misery to describe and a wonder to behold.' Most people revert to Darwin, who deduced that coral builds up around a submerged volcano, producing something called a fringing reef. The island then starts to sink, but the coral continues to grow upwards. Eventually the island vanishes completely, leaving only the circle of coral around the lagoon – layer upon layer of it. The *Oxford English Dictionary* is more direct: '*atoll* . . . Ring-shaped coral reef enclosing lagoon'.

Some of the island names were familiar to me – the

Carolines, Yap, Truk, Ponape, the Marianas – but Palau wasn't. There are over two thousand islands in Micronesia and, despite being called 'micro', the entire region of ocean and islands is about equal in area to the United States.

Over the years, various powers – Germany, Spain and Japan – have left their mark of occupation on Micronesia, and today the islands are a direct and crucial part of the American military system. It is America's military and economic might that has shaped them.

It was in the Micronesian Marshall Islands that America tested more than sixty-five atomic bombs on Bikini and Eniwetok atolls during the fifties and early sixties. While pulverizing the atolls on the one hand, the United States has spent billions of dollars with the other, developing Kwajalein atoll as part of the Star Wars tracking system and relocating the islanders who lived there on to yet another atoll, Ebeye, the slum of the Pacific.

Between the two World Wars Micronesia came under Japanese control. The Japanese built roads, hospitals, harbours and airports, all of which were reduced to rubble by American bombing during the war in the Pacific. In the Western Pacific, Palau was taken from the Japanese after some of the bloodiest fighting of the war. When it was finally all over, the United Nation's designated Micronesia a trust territory, to be governed by the United States. And so, in 1947, the Carolines, the Marianas and the Marshalls all became US trusteeships.

Most people remember the 'winds of change' blowing through Africa, but they blew through the Pacific too. During the sixties, colonialism was an unpopular word and the former colonial powers began to divest themselves of their territories. President Kennedy sent a mission to the region to recommend a new Pacific policy for America's trust territories that would be more in keeping with the sentiments of that time. The resulting report, the Solomon Report, was a masterpiece of contradiction. America wanted to retain control of Micronesia and planned ways in which the manipulation of economic aid could influence the way islands might vote in future. Yes, the trusteeships must have independence, but they must also be brought into a 'permanent relationship' with the USA. In short, the Report stated the impossibility of true independence for Micronesia and worked towards ways in which a special association might be created which would give a reasonable appearance of self-government. America's trusteeship was to be replaced by a new political relationship called the 'Compact of Free Association'.

The Compact is a complex 'strategic defense' document. Its most relevant features are that it effectively gives the USA the right to intervene in the islands' affairs, seize land and have exclusive use of the islands for harbours, air-force bases and jungle-warfare training. At the same time, the Compact frees the United States of any responsibility for the health and well-being of the islanders. In other words, it purchases an island's sovereignty and autonomy in exchange for financial subsidies.

★

A chill fog blew in from the Channel and hung over Folkestone's main street. There was a damp and dismal cold. In his office, above a car showroom, Barrie Thompson led me through the intricate series of killings and fire bombings that had taken place on Palau and sketched out to me the British connection. My producer friend had been right – it was a hell of a story.

During the seventies, when the first real steps of North Pacific decolonization were being undertaken, most people in the US Administration thought that all the Micronesian islands would group together as one political unit. But they didn't. The Northern Marianas voted to become a commonwealth of the USA. Yap, Truk, Ponape and Kosrae, in the Carolines, became the Federated States of Micronesia, or FSM. Guam decided to remain a US territory, and the Marshall Islands and Palau decided to become republics.

In their first act of self-determination, the Palauans

rejected US citizenship and framed a nuclear-free constitution barring nuclear, chemical and toxic weapons from the island – which was perhaps unfortunate for some of the planners in Washington, because Palau has the only Pacific deep-water harbour capable of housing nuclear submarines outside Subic Bay in the Philippines, and nobody knew which way the Philippines would fall. The United States vetoed Palau's new constitution and forced nine elections on the issue. Each time the United States framed new amendments to their constitution, the Palauans threw them out. Each time the Palauans voted against accepting the Compact, somebody got killed or fire-bombed. There were also those in Washington who felt the same way, and somewhere in the middle of all this there was the Ipseco involvement, underwritten by a consortium of British bankers.

In May 1983 a British company, Ipseco – International Power Systems – signed a contract with Palau to build a power plant on the island. Palau paid $32 million for the plant, twice as much as its annual budget. The plant's capacity was far in excess of the needs of Palau's fifteen thousand people. Ipseco's President, Gordon Mochrie, assured the Palauan Government that the project would eventually pay for itself through the sales of electricity and fuel. Within a year, the island had defaulted on its first payment and was bankrupt. The banking syndicate which had floated the loan sued Palau. Palau claimed that the plant was incomplete and counter-sued Ipseco. Another year later, Ipseco was declared bankrupt and liquidators were appointed. In the labyrinthine politics that followed, and indeed are still going on, several people have been murdered, including the Palauan President, and the United States Administration has been heavily implicated in what some people have described as a major conspiracy to do with nuclear bases.

Into this internecine squabble – international conspiracy or local clan warfare, the definition varying according to whose side you're on – walked Barrie Thompson.

Thompson was unimpressed with Palau and the Palauans. He had expected beautiful islands and friendly women, or the other way round – women with almond eyes and waist-length tresses, Gauguinesque, not the smaller and stockier Palauans. Thompson didn't like the island either, not keen on mangrove swamps and disgusted by its politics. He was to become even more disgusted with what his investigations uncovered both there and, later, in Washington; a network of corruption going to some very high places – so high, a less confident man would have dropped his investigation then and there. But somewhere in the middle of all this was Thompson's prey: Gordon Mochrie, the President of Ipseco.

The British company had not only built the power plant and bankrupted the country but was now implicated in bribery and fraud. It was also about to build a further five power plants on a further five small islands in Micronesia. Thompson was determined to get a settlement for his Palestinian client, who had invested £50,000 and was expecting in return one-third of the anticipated profits. Thompson assessed the anticipated profits to be somewhere in the region of $7 million. When confronted with this figure, Mochrie laughed and said, 'You're nearly right. In fact, I owe your client $9.6 million.'

While he was in Palau, its Government asked Thompson to make his findings available to them, and at this point Mochrie stepped in with a High Court action to prevent him from talking, even though, as he was working for the Palauan Government, Thompson had privilege. The day before Thompson was due to face Gordon Mochrie in the High Court, his solicitor informed him that President Remelik of Palau had been assassinated in a Chicago-gangland-style killing. For the first time, Barrie Thompson had some idea of the Byzantine nature of Palauan politics. As we lunched in an Indian restaurant frequented by former cronies from the Kent police, Thompson – normally a slightly cocky man – admitted that he had, for the first time, felt really scared.

Palau's President, Haruo Remelik, had been shot down outside his house late one Saturday night. As he got out of his car, the killers were waiting. They forced him into some bushes behind his house and shot him several times in the head and body, then got away.

The Palauan police, together with the FBI, investigated the murder, but were unable to recover any weapons or even to determine the make of the gun used. In fact, no evidence of any kind was uncovered that might give a clue to the assassins' identify. However, four young men were arrested and charged, including the son and the nephew of the dead President's chief political rival, a leading candidate in the forthcoming presidential election. He was forced to stand down, leaving the succession to the presidency open to two other candidates. One of them was Lazarus Salii – Palau's 'ambassador' to the Compact of Free Association negotiations with the United States, and ardently pro the agreement.

Back in London after my lunch with Thompson, I sought out a decent map of the Pacific. I then rang my travel agent, Don Cleary, a skinny, charming Irishman. Don has a patience that borders on saintliness and, although he spends most of his time moving big business around the world, for some inexplicable reason he is prepared to take time out to cope with the indecisiveness and vagaries of people like myself whose budgets don't usually match up to their ambitions. No armchair traveller, when Don wants to relax he treks through the Himalayas. He suggested lunch and that I contact a couple of airlines for some kind of concessionary ticket. I mapped out a route, not helped by the fact that, since their nominal independence, many of the Micronesian islands had changed their names. The airline guides hadn't caught up with that. Was Palau 'Palau' or 'Belau', and what was the name of the capital? There was no room on my map for the capital cities of small Pacific islands. Somewhere we found it – Koror. Then the Marshalls. Were they part of the Carolines? Ponape had become Pohnpei. But that was the island – its capital was Kolonia. I had lived in the Pacific for almost two years, but these islands were completely new to me.

Don went back to the airline guide and I went back to try charming the two better-known airlines that fly the Pacific. Neither was in the mood to be charmed, although Continental suggested that it might be able to help with a route, as it did fly between most of the places I wanted to visit. However, the travel clerk I was rerouted to on the phone was less than helpful. Apart from a general unfamiliarity with the islands, which was perhaps unsurprising, there was the unreasonable assumption on my part that because the airline flew there he would know where places were.

He was emphatic: 'The places you want to go don't connect at all.'

'Of course they connect,' I said irritably. 'I've got your route map in front of me. Have you got the Marshalls? Well then, go down a bit, west, then south, there's Ponape – well, it's Pohnpei now. From there I want to go . . .'

I could almost see him shrug his shoulders at the end of the phone.

'They don't connect,' he said pointedly. 'You have to fly back to Hawaii and connect out.'

'But that'd cost a fortune.'

That was not his problem.

Ned Friary and Glenda Bendure's *Travel Survival Guide* put it quite succinctly. 'Gateways to Micronesia,' they said, 'include Honolulu, Guam, Japan, Manila, Hong Kong, Bali, Nauru, Fiji and Kiribati. Travellers coming from elsewhere,' they said firmly, 'need to first find their way to one of these connections.'

I rang Don again. 'Well,' he said cheerfully, 'I can get you to Hawaii cheaply. Perhaps you'd better try and make your own way from there.'

★

Weeks later, high up on New York's smart East Side, the

air-conditioners were working overtime.

'I'm confused,' I said. 'I don't understand whether this new Compact has been approved or not approved.' Under Palauan law, changes to the constitution require acceptance by a seventy-five per cent vote. The New and Improved Compact of Free Association, as it had optimistically been renamed, had never obtained the required seventy-five per cent, yet the Palauan Government and President Lazarus Salii were saying it was agreed. A further change in their constitution had decreed that the margin of acceptance was now fifty per cent, and fifty per cent of the population had apparently voted yes to the 'new and improved' agreement with the United States. As a thank-you, the Americans were to provide an aid package worth $18 million a year for fifteen years. In return, America was to get exclusive use of Palau for harbours, air-force bases and jungle training. Palauans could also take up US citizenship.

Could the President change the constitution just like that? 'That's being debated in Palau's Supreme Court at this moment,' said David Richenthal. Tanned and sleek, Richenthal had represented three of the four young men accused of assassinating President Remelik. Charges against the fourth had mysteriously been dropped. The others had finally been acquitted.

'It's not surprising you're confused,' Richenthal said, 'There was an attempt to amend the constitution, to change the seventy-five per cent to fifty per cent. That was on the seventh and eight Plebiscite. Then a lawsuit was filed to challenge the legality of the constitutional amendment process. One of the island chiefs, Yatuka Gibbons, had started it, but then he withdrew it.'

I had heard of Gibbons: he had been a prime mover in opposing the Ipseco deal. At the time when the deal went through, there had been no competitive bidding. That, like a lot of other things, was contrary to the Palauan constitution. Gibbons, who was a high chief, brought a lawsuit against President Remelik alleging that, had the plant been open to tender, it would have cost more like $15 million, not $32 million, and that it was illegal. It had, he alleged, been procured by bribery. Shortly after filing the lawsuit, the Chief's attorney was fire-bombed and had fled to Hawaii. The lawsuit was dropped.

'Why did Gibbons drop this second lawsuit?' I asked.

'Well, it seems possible that he received a $100,000 pay-off,' smiled Richenthal. 'I tell you, Palauan politics are Byzantine.'

And why had Remelik been assassinated? That was complicated too.

It seems that, when the Ipseco deal was put forward, various people spoke out against it. It was far in excess of Palau's needs; there hadn't been 'full and fair competition' in the handing out of the tender; the Government would never be able to meet the debt-service requirements on the loan . . . but Remelik signed the deal anyway. The island's subsequent bankruptcy and rumours of backhanders precipitated a major political crisis. According to another attorney, who had also fled to Hawaii, Remelik was planning to come clean in a TV speech to the nation, reveal bribery and fraud, repudiate the loans, establish a legal defence and save the economy of his island, but he was killed the day before the speech. Was he killed to prevent him from going public?

'Anyway,' said Richenthal, 'Gibbon's original lawsuit was picked up by the women elders, but that too was withdrawn because of intimidation. Then it was filed again in April, and this is the suit that is still being litigated.'

'What happens if they win?'

'It's back to square one,' he said.

'Look,' he said, 'probably the only predictable thing is the unpredictability of this part of the world. There's an election in November, same as ours. It's possible somebody will put up another constitutional amendment. Dukakis and Bush hold very different policies concerning Micronesia.' He started to pace the floor. I felt like joining him.

'How did you become involved?' I asked. 'What are the

mechanics that a successful New York attorney gets to defend three young men on a desert island thousands of miles away?'

'Well, I knew nothing about the politics of it all,' said Richenthal. 'I did it because my partner couldn't. He's married to a Palauan and too close personally to the defendants, who are relatives by marriage. It's an interesting case legally.' He paused. 'It really is a colony, you know. It doesn't have jury trials, even though it's an American territory. That's what got me out there in the first case. I must say I had my eyes opened.'

I remembered reading that the boys he defended were tried without jury. The whole prosecution sounded a farce. An eyewitness, a woman with the unlikely name of Mysteca Maidesil, a former girlfriend of two of the accused, was suddenly produced from nowhere. Having started her story by declaring that somebody from Guam had killed the President, she then told the police that she had heard the suspects discussing how they were going to kill him, and that one of them had confessed to her the day after the murder. Maidesil changed her story four times altogether; however, it was on the basis of her evidence that the defendants were originally convicted and sentenced to thirty-five years. After their conviction, they applied to the Appelate Division of the Supreme Court of Palau for bail. The court was told about the extraordinary trial proceedings and all three justices granted the bail, which was an indication of the weakness of the case against the accused and the complexity of the circumstances surrounding the murder. If they really were believed guilty of a presidential assassination, it would seem foolhardy to permit three convicted assassins to go free on bail.

'It's a town without a sheriff,' said Richenthal – 'there's just no law in town.' He looked serious for a moment. 'You know, they weren't only acquitted: they were innocent. I don't want people saying "Well, he was a smart-arsed East Coast lawyer who got them off." After two years, you've got to get something right.'

I liked him for that.

★

'It sounds to me like a dictatorship up for grabs, cloaked in the garb of democracy and all put in a glowing light by the US Government,' said a friend from Washington when I endeavoured to sketch out to him the salient features of the Palau story. He was coming along. When I had last seen him, he had thought the Contras were fighting for democracy in Central America!

I was fresh from the Congressional hearings where a House Subcommittee on Insular and International Affairs was holding up the ratification of the Compact by Congress. Congressional hearings are like a piece of theatre, but played more for the participants than for the audience. The stage was set by three uniformed janitors wheeling in a massive filing-cabinet and then two trolleys full of cardboard boxes. By lunchtime, the floor surrounding the Representatives' podium and beyond looked like Napoleon's headquarters at the Battle of Waterloo. The drawers of the cabinet had spilled over as files, letters and documents were produced in evidence and counter-evidence. At three o'clock the porters would manhandle the whole lot back on to the trolleys and up to the thirteenth floor. This had been going on for months and one of the Congressional aides was predicting it would continue into 1989.

Once I had managed to cut through the rhetoric of democracy, it seemed that the purpose of the hearings was not to uncover and determine those in the Administration responsible for the corruption and malpractice in Palau but rather to have a kind of outward and visible sign of American democracy at work.

Under the chairmanship of Ron de Lugo – a bespectacled, wry man – the House Interior and Insular Affairs Committee was resisting approval of the Compact until assured that it was what the Palauans wanted and what the United States wanted and that it would go through the correct constitutional processes to get implemented. As far as what the Palauans wanted was concerned, prosecution and defence were merely arguing 'How much?' – the Committee was looking into the right things, but for the wrong reasons.

Although I rather liked him, de Lugo too was choosing the wrong solution – to throw more money at the problem. The question was how much money. The State Department was happy to provide Palau with an aid package of $428 million, out of which it expected Palau to be able to pay off the Ipseco debt. De Lugo's committee wanted this increased by an extra $32 million specifically to cover the Ipseco debt. The State Department – in the shape of two men in grey suits, Berg and Hills – felt that to pick up the Ipseco bill was to 'infringe Palau's sovereignty'. This was an extraordinary statement. Palau's sovereignty was now wrapped up in an aid package in which Palauans had lost their lands, many people had lost their lives, and the entire island had become dependent on American welfare. Here were two representatives from the State department – both attorneys, government functionaries – talking without a blush about the possibility of Palau's losing its sovereignty!

De Lugo started to list years of mismanagement of America's trusteeship. The island, it appeared, was now a main centre for the trans-shipment of heroin. Of Palau's fifteen thousand people, four hundred were heroin addicts. Marijuana had become a major export. Palau was the only Micronesian state that hadn't got a new hospital – the existing one had a leaking roof and the X-ray machine was fifteen years old. There was no functional plumbing.

'We should be proud of ourselves,' said de Lugo, peering over his glasses.

Then there was the matter of the public auditor, or rather the absence of a public auditor. How was the United States able to gauge whether the Government of Palau was properly spending and accounting for its federal expenditure without an audit? There had been a $1 million payment from Ipseco to three Palauan officials, among them the President, Lazarus Salii. They said they had received the money for legitimate business and political purposes. 'How, then,' de Lugo sighed, 'did it find its way into the President's Hong Kong bank account?' The island had no funds left for staffing an auditor's office. Anyway, the last auditor was subjected to 'political pressure' and had left the country in a hurry, under escort.

The catalogue of corruption and inefficiencies went on. It seemed that, even with the Ipseco plant functioning – which it wasn't – not all of Palau would receive power. 'Corruption isn't responsible for all Palau's problems,' mumbled one of the men from the State Department.

There was also, said de Lugo, the question of someone close to President Salii who was implicated in the murder of the father of a prominent Palauan lawyer who had been representing an anti-Compact group. De Lugo leaned back and threw his arms open. 'Don't we ever get any of these murders solved out there?' he asked plaintively.

The litany continued. How was it that the Ministry of Social Services had been told to instruct teachers to campaign for the Compact and to submit the names of those who didn't support it to the President's office?

A cool cat in a lightweight suit took the stand: James Berg, Director of the Office of Freely Associated State Affairs within the State Department.

He agreed that the Compact might not be perfect. The trusteeship agreement had been flawed: it didn't allow the people of Palau to chart their own course. 'But when we negotiated the Compact, we negotiated it to suit the interests of the USA. We weren't negotiating for Palau, we were negotiating for the United States. The government of Palau deserves credit,' said Berg, 'for the way in which law and order have been restored. I wish Palau would be left alone by outsiders so that their system would work,' he said rather fervently.

'Aw come off it, fellas. The rule of law is illusory,' said de Lugo, leaning back in his chair. 'Don't you think,' he asked patiently, 'that these things ought to be independently looked into? What's going on out there?'

The man from the State Department stammered a little. De Lugo became adamant. The US shouldn't be subsidizing the subversion of law and order in Palau and, until both an auditor and a public prosecutor were appointed, the aid money should be put in trust.

The State Department's man made allegations of outside interference in Palau's affair by do-gooders – a reference to Greenpeace and the American Civil Liberties Union.

De Lugo balked at this. 'What about agitation from the inside? Who was dragged out of his house at midnight and told to legislate a new Constitution? That's a hell of a way to legislate,' he drawled, peering over his spectacles again. He had the mannerism down to a fine art. And just how would the current Palauan Government 'acquire' for Compact use – in other words, military use – land that was held privately by Palauans who might be anti-Compact, asked de Lugo.

The US just wanted to use the land, not to acquire it, maintained the State Department. How the land was acquired was an internal matter.

'And who can verify that the positions of the auditor and prosecutor will be maintained over the next fifteen years?' asked de Lugo.

And if they are not, how do you prosecute the President, and friends of the President, I thought?

Later I talked with one of the members of de Lugo's committee. 'Our members want the Compact,' he said, 'because the majority want it. It's embarrassing to be a trusteeship in 1988. We want bases, We're unsure about the Philippines, and we don't want this nuclear-free disease to spread. We're pro-Compact and anti-corruption. They're not going to get their Compact without these things being looked into.'

After all, he went on, a great deal of the $460 million being talked about was American taxpayers' money. He referred to Salii as a 'Mini-Marcos'. This Administration wanted the Compact to get through before November because Fred

Zeder was close to Bush – and it was election time.

Fred Zeder had been the US Ambassador to Micronesia at the time of the Ipseco negotiations. He was a Reagan appointee and a good friend of Gordon Mochrie – such a good friend that, when the syndicate of London banks was about to turn down Palau's loan request for the $32 million to finance the Ipseco plant, it was Zeder who sent a telex from Washington urging the banks to go ahead with the funding and assuring them that the Administration wanted to encourage the Ipseco project. Zeder was now handling Bush's financial affairs in Hawaii and Micronesia. He was tipped for office if Bush were to get the presidency.[1]

Zeder had told the Washington columnist Jack Anderson, 'I think the Pacific is a great place to do business. The Pacific needs help, but not from a bunch of bureaucrats who don't know a thing about economic development.'

Anderson had been having a field-day with Palau, describing the machinations there as 'a series of financial boondoggles'. One of the most recently uncovered of these was a scheme whereby Palauan passports were on offer in Hong Kong for a quarter of a million dollars each. Palauan nationality automatically guarantees citizenship of the United States, an attractive proposition to drug dealers, and even businessmen, from the Far East. The Palauan Government was to take twelve per cent of the profits – a novel way, perhaps of paying off the Ipseco debt.

I went to see one of the State Department's despised 'do-gooding' agencies, Greenpeace. The co-ordinator of Greenpeace's Pacific Campaign is Sebia Hawkins, a small, dark-eyed lady as bright as she is beautiful. 'Ah,' she said, eyeing me. 'I saw you at the hearing yesterday. I was wondering who you were. You either get the CIA or the military at those things,' she said, 'and you obviously weren't the military.'

Surprisingly, she was not into conspiracy theories on the Palau issue. 'I guess the importance of the Pacific to the

States right now is more of strategic denial,' she said. 'We still have secure bases. Although the integrity of the agreement with the Philippines and a couple of other places is being challenged, I still think, for the moment anyway, the United States does feel fairly secure about maintaining their Pacific presence. That could all change within a moment. In broader terms,' she continued, 'the greater interest of the United States is to ensure that the Soviet Union or the Chinese don't make inroads militarily into the region, but it's becoming increasingly difficult to the Department of Defense and the United States to argue with any credibility that the Soviets have a significant naval presence in the Pacific, especially the South-West Pacific. The only argument that the United States can continue to make politically with any credibility in the region is that they want to maintain the *status quo* militarily.'

Unsurprisingly, she was scathing about the Compact of Free Association. 'It's not free at all,' she said. 'It's a way for the United States acquiring greater control over Micronesia. I don't think it's as co-ordinated as a conspiracy because I don't think the US Government is that co-ordinated. I don't think there's a single monolith that's always in control – I think it's a bit more haywire and a bit more chaotic than a lot of people presume. But it's clear for historic reasons, maybe emotional reasons, maybe psychological reasons, as well as strategic reasons, that the US Government is not going to let go of Micronesia. It's not "free association" at all. To me it epitomizes the total absence of democracy being fostered in Micronesia. They have never been offered a genuine choice about the political status they want to assume.'

She underpinned the doubts I had felt during the hearings. The USA was fostering a total dependency. The only thing under discussion was the nature of that dependency: commonwealth status or free association, whatever they might mean, but never independence.

'That is, as far as I'm concerned, no choice,' said Sebia, 'They're offered $450 million or nothing. That's it. The concept of free association is purely a semantic ploy.'

'The thing that strikes me the most,' she said, 'is that, from the very beginning of the negotiations to get out of trusteeship, the key or principal figures involved in the negotiations have been businessmen. I'm not saying that it's bad or wrong,' she said, with a frown that belied her words; 'however, it's clear that in Micronesia the largest special interests at work in the history of this "evolving relationship" have been outside business interests who have been involved in the negotiations purely for personal enrichment.'

The linking of American business interests to Palau's path to political independence would certainly be a cause for concern in most First World governments, where it is considered unseemly to have too many connections between business and politics. The number of Americans who had been working on the Micronesian negotiations and were now working for Ipseco was legion, and they were commonly known as the 'Micronesian job network'.

Although existing US legislation is intended to prevent officials working on the negotiations lobbying the Administration on behalf of private interests, it had fallen short of preventing them hand-picking certain Palauans for office and being able to reap the rewards later.

'Those individuals who have negotiated foreign policy and ensured Micronesia remains permanently attached to the USA are the same individuals who are enriching themselves through corporate schemes,' Sebia was emphatic. 'That's happening throughout the Pacific, and has happened in the Pacific since 1946.'

And longer, I thought. There used to be seven hundred American whalers working the Pacific. I thought of the trading companies with their ruthless acquisition of land; of the Catholic mission in Papua New Guinea selling copra from its huge estates; of the report I had read prophesying how Guam could develop into a second Hong Kong, given freedom from 'over-regulation'.

My eyes fell on one of Greenpeace's beautiful posters of

a dugong, now threatened by the world's sophisticated fishing habits. My mind grasshoppered to fishing. 'What about the Japanese? All that tuna fishing?' I asked.

She groaned. 'If you look at every single environmental problem in the Pacific, it can be traced back to Japan one way or another. Look at rain-forest devastation; look at proposals to store nuclear waste in the sea bed; look at toxic-chemical dumping; look at pesticide use; look at consumption of fossil fuels; look at marine-mammal slaughter and overfishing – Japan's there. This whole Rising Sun thing over the Pacific is a real serious one – and culturally difficult, because Japan is so impossible to deal with.'

'What do you mean by that?'

'They're impossible for Westerners to deal with. They confuse Westerners because they treat them as barbarians. It's very, very difficult for Westerners, whether they be diplomats or activists, to know how to develop a Japan policy. On the surface the Japanese are incredibly polite and wonderful and gracious, but when you hit the bottom line the bottom line is that Westerners, occidentals, are racially inferior. I'm not arguing the rights and wrongs of that. It's just that Westerners react to that because it's usually them – us – who have institutionalized racism. And they don't know how to deal with reverse racism.'

'None of us do. But how do you stop an entire nation's eating habits?'

'I don't know. I'm seriously wondering about a "boycott chopsticks" campaign. When you think of the decimation of the rain-forests in Papua New Guinea and Indonesia, going to disposable chopsticks. It's very difficult to deal with Japan, yet they have to be dealt with because of their involvement in so many of the serious issues facing the Pacific.'

So how do new governments of small island nations, in dire need of foreign exchange, legislate and then monitor these countries? I wondered. There are no internal political structures for monitoring environmental degradation from logging, reef-dredging, mining. They don't have the political legislation or a tradition of officially protecting the environment, because it's always been a cultural or family function to take care of the land. And many of them don't even have the will any more.

'No,' said Sebia, 'And, even if they have the political structure and the will, they don't have the personnel. Look they're not going to have an island in fifty years if they don't develop some kind of environment consciousness. That's not to say that you throw out every single mining or logging proposal but that you recognize that, being tiny fragile states, with the exception of Papua New Guinea, they do not have the same time within which to develop unsoundly. They're not continental, they're not huge like the United States or Australia or India. They have to be convinced that individually they have to assess what their future needs are going to be and develop appropriately and sustainably.

'Do you know,' she said, 'that in the Solomons at the moment they have between fifty-two and fifty-six mining proposals and there are only two people to handle them and, between the two of them, to evaluate each of those proposals soundly, then monitor the development proposals and monitor the development itself, and then to regulate it! It's impossible.'

'You know, one of the problems with the Pacific is that there's a total absence of information about it. And that's the nature of Oceania. She is a vast area. She's very mysterious and she's very fantastic, and most people imagine her in this Gauguinish day dream as the escape paradise from the crazy hectic Northern Western world. And, unless you get out there and spend some time travelling, you have no idea what's really happening out there. These are fragile tiny little ecosystems – amazing ecosystems, but very fragile. If you tip your balance you're going to look like Nauru[2] in a few years. That's all there is to it.'

'In other words,' I said, 'they have no choice.'

Sebia shook her head. 'No choice.'

Chapter 5

WESTERN SAMOA

THE LAST EARTHLY PARADISE

The departure lounge at Honolulu Airport was peopled by giants: great golden-skinned people in party mood, their sleek black hair pulled back off big-boned, strong faces. Children rushed around garlanded in candy leis. Everybody knew everybody. I realized how long I had been away from the real Pacific. As I checked in, the Hawaiian Airlines representative said with surprise, 'Apia? That's primitive. Whaddya wanna go there for?' I knew I had made the right decision.

The Samoans had not an angle on their big, rounded bodies. On the plane, the woman sitting next to me overlapped into my seat. She was vast. She put one great leg under each of the seats in front of her. I sat fixed, unable to move for the next five hours. She ate her dinner then her daughter's, and smiled at me benignly.

Only a few of us scampered off into the wooden arrivals shed at three in the morning. The air was soft and sweet. It was a perfect Pacific night under a dense black sky with a thousand stars cascading into the lagoon. Of all the islands in the Pacific I had always wanted to come here and I knew I wasn't going to be disappointed.

Apia was cool and rainswept, and the immigration officer who stamped my passport said, 'Thank you, Cherry.' Outside the wooden terminal building, a brightly painted bus waited, festooned with airline, tour and hotel stickers from everywhere around the world. Someone threw my bags on to the bus and then did the same with me.

A young man in the seat in front introduced himself. He worked, he said, at the Bureau of Statistics and was returning from a conference in Guam. He had been flying across the Pacific for about three days, first to Hawaii, now home. Despite his tiredness, he was exuberant about the experience. 'Anything you need to know,' he said – 'any tables, population figures, growth rates – my office is at the side of the Prime Minister's office. I'm Danny. Just come and ask for me.'

I tried to think of a statistic I might need and settled on one I already knew – population.

'About 164,000 right now,' said Danny. 'Samoa has a declining growth rate; that's mostly due to migration.' But it was too late, or too early, to dream up intelligent questions.

Danny had been educated in New Zealand but, unlike many of his fellow-Samoans, had come back.

Outside the terminal, a young German couple nervously asked the bus fare into town and then checked it in a guidebook. It was twenty-five miles into Apia, and there wasn't a taxi in sight. Someone cheerfully threw the Germans' luggage on to the bus. Uncheerfully, the man boarded the bus and took it off again. The girl came on to the bus and asked me the fare, so I asked Danny. 'Four tala,' he said – 'two dollars.' The man carried their bags back on to the bus.

I could just make out the lagoon on our left as we wound through the coconut groves. Sometimes a light had been left on and I could glimpse under the trees the skeletal insides of a fale, the uniquely beehive-shaped Samoan thatched hut. The huts had no walls, just supports for the oval roofs. Days later, when I lay in one gazing upwards, I saw what a glorious and intricate network of ribs and beams these roofs were, with no nails ever used.

The fales were raised off the ground, and inside I could see a kind of clutter of chairs and the odd sideboard. In one, strange and ghostly, a white mosquito net cascaded to the floor, under it the outline of a sleeping body. I thought, there has to be something right with a society which has no doors and no windows and where people can sleep in the open.

Danny got off somewhere between the airport and Apia. He waved sleepily and said, 'See you at Statistics.' Later the bus stopped at a motel opposite a brightly lit white building with a gilded golden angel on top of it blowing a trumpet, the Mormon Temple.

Finally, at the other end of town, we fell out on to the pavement at 'the most famous two words in the Pacific,' – Aggie Greys – and smiling girls and boys in lava-lavas helped with bags and pre-dawn irritability.

An old man courteously showed me along a path lined with crotons and washed with rain. In the room there was a familiar smell, yeasty and comforting. It had formed part of my life somewhere before. Sniffing, I went round the room, inside damp cupboards and drawers. Not until I crawled into bed and smelled it on the sheets did it come back to me. It was the smell of my old house in Papua New Guinea after years of spraying against cockroaches and insects – a combination of the wood, damp and humidity. I must have fallen asleep with a broad and contented smile on my face.

I was woken a few hours later by a loud knocking and, without waiting for a reply, the housemaid charged in through the door. Her face was testimony to Thor Heyerdahl's thesis. Small, with great flat cheek-bones and a copper skin, her genes had definitely started out in Peru or Bolivia. I crept away from her chattering, back along the path to Aggie's front step to take in the morning.

So many words have been written about Aggie Grey and her hotel that they have now taken on the stuff of legend. I have never entirely believed the mythologies that have grown up around the place and the over-enthusiastic efforts to present it in its earlier days as a sanctum of respectability, which unarguably it is today. Aggie made her name, fame and fortune during the war by providing all the comforts of home to the American forces stationed

in the Pacific. Today, family, fans and the odd hagio-
grapher insist that those comforts went only so far as the
supply of cold beer, French fries and hamburgers to the
hungry GIs. But Aggie was a shrewd businesswoman and
she also made sure that only the prettiest girls in Samoa
were on hand to serve them. Given the influence of the
church in the islands and a tough traditional village
system, maybe the service did stop short at French fries;
but given the nature of GIs and the charm of the Samoan
girls, it's hard to believe.

Aggie herself was the daughter of an English chemist
who came to Samoa from New Zealand and married a
local girl. His wife died very young, but not, however,
before she had given birth to three daughters: Aggie,
Maggie and Mary. Aggie married twice, was widowed
twice and had seven children. She opened her hotel when
times were hard, and acquired a lasting reputation for
herself when James Michener supposedly modelled his
character 'Bloody Mary' on her in *Tales from the South
Pacific*. She spent most of her later years denying it, but no
publicity is bad publicity and business has been booming
ever since. Testament to it is the ominously large new wing
now being added to what was still a pleasantly casual,
ramshackle wooden building on the waterfront.

In sunlight, Apia looked inviting. The small white town
sat on the curve of the bay, its main road lined with low
wooden buildings on the land side. Most of them, it
appeared, were something to do with the church, if not
churches themselves: the Protestant church, the Congregational church, the Protestant church hall, then the
Catholic cathedral, all-imposing and white cement. Down
the road a few steps was the High Court, at the side
of which was Danny's office, white clapboard with a
verandah running round it. There were a couple of
uninteresting-looking bars with inappropriate-sounding
names – The Love Boat and Otto's Reef – and, further
down, a blue-painted wooden shack giving out a hot yeast
smell, a real one this time. A bakery, the kiosk was selling

fresh bread. On the waterfront side of the road there was an assortment of painted wooden shacks selling tinned corned beef and soft drinks. In the steaming glass cases, hot meat-pies sat and shrivelled in the sun.

All roads seemed to run back from Apia's sea-front to the hills at the back, covered in dense green rain forest. It was on one of these mountains, Mount Vaea, that Robert Louis Stevenson had lived and died.

★

'It's the only high-rise in town, opposite the library – you won't miss it,' Bob Barlow had said on the phone. A cheerful New Zealander, Bob was acting British Honorary Consul. 'High-rise' meant two storeys, and he was right, it did stick out. I liked him immediately, not least because he was faintly rude about the nature of Margaret Mead's studies in Samoa. He'd been in Samoa for twelve years, and it was obvious that he loved the place.

'They're going to have to do something soon about universal suffrage,' he said. 'The matai system can't continue. The political system has polluted the matai system; it must break down, because now they are only voting titles.'

From village to national level in Western Samoa, authority is still vested in the matai or elders. Each village is an extended family – the aiga – and each aiga has one or more matai at its head. To be a matai is to hold a position of privilege and prestige. The matai have power over land use and wealth. They control not only the land but also the economic and social decisions within the village. Only the matai can vote in the national elections. Appointed by the aiga, they were once chosen for their accumulated wisdom and knowledge – it would have been rare to find a matai under forty. It still is, but whether they are voted in for their knowledge as opposed to their power has become a contentious issue.

I asked Bob how he'd come here. 'As a lawyer,' he replied – 'Company law mostly.' He hadn't wanted to get involved in criminal law. Too much of a softie, I thought.

'The most beautiful thing about this place', he said, 'is the strength of the traditional system here. They have this fungu system. I had a case, a girl who had been raped. The family came to see me; they had witnesses, the girl knew the boy. It was all going along as normal; then, as the trial date drew nearer and nearer, people started hanging back. Eye-witnesses started to contradict themselves. That was when I found out. Under the traditional system, what happens is that the boy's family will go to the girl's family taking gifts – cans of corned beef, bananas, that sort of thing. And they take fine mats and they put them on their heads and sit outside the fale. The aggrieved family will come outside and curse them, call them names, generally heap scorn upon them. But they'll just keep sitting there in silence.'

'A kind of public atonement,' I said. 'But where's the boy in all this. Is he with them?'

'No, not necessarily,' said Bob. 'He's probably sitting under a coconut drinking beer and not in the least sorry for what he's done. It can go on for days, but eventually the family of the girl will invite them in and they will accept the gifts and they will eat together and the bonds between the two families will be stronger in the future for it.'

'Is there a death penalty here?'

'The death sentence is mandatory here in the case of murder, but it's never been carried out. Nobody would want blood on their hands. It's always been revoked by the head of state.'

'Have you read Albert Wendt?' Bob suddenly asked. I hadn't. 'Samoan writer. He's in New Zealand now. You should read him. He's married to a palagi, a white. He writes about identity crisis, culture shock.' He started rifling through a bookshelf.

I remembered reading somewhere that Samoa has one of the highest literacy rates in the world. Samoans have been called 'the Italians of the Pacific', and pride themselves on their gifts of oratory and poetry. A matai, said Bob, can be appointed for his gift of oratory – a Talking Chief. He finished rifling.

'There's a good collection in the library across the road – the Pacific collection. It's worth having a nose round,' Bob said. 'Anything you want, just call.' Then he added, 'Just keep your eyes and ears open. You won't miss much.'

Outside, the sun was hot and hard and blinding. It was still only half past nine. I needed shade and relief from the light. On the sea side of the road stood a low white building, the Nelson Library. The Pacific collection was closed as they hadn't enough staff to keep it open, the girl behind the desk said, but it would be possible to open it by appointment. Perhaps Saturday. I made an appointment and then browsed round the one large, light room that housed everything else. Fans whirred noisily overhead, and the wooden tables were crammed with schoolchildren reading and writing intensely. The books were the odd collection that you often get where there is an expatriate colony: a history of Chelsea Football Club; a series called *Living without . . .* – including *Living without Gloves*. Outside, the traffic slowly negotiated one of Apia's three roundabouts and the gaudily painted local buses, open at the sides where the windows should be, played pop music very loudly. I wondered how the matai would keep the young people in the villages and, if tourism was developed, how they would keep the tourists happy and the people intact at the same time?

★

Rupert Brooke said about Samoa

> You lie on a mat in a cool Samoan hut and look out on the white sand under the high palms and a gentle sea and the black line of the reef a mile out and moonlight over everything. And then among it all are the loveliest people in the world moving and dancing like Gods and Goddesses. It is sheer beauty so pure it is difficult to breathe in it.

Brooke wasn't the only writer to come here and fall in love. Robert Louis Stevenson made Samoa his home, became enmeshed in its politics and eventually died here. I began to feel as though I were following Stevenson on his travels, island by island. He had spent time in Tahiti and Hawaii and was a great favourite of the Hawaiian royal family. I had seen some wonderful photographs of a younger Stevenson, skinny and tubercular, being entertained by King Kalakaua at a Polynesian feast and telling stories to the young princesses. Now his house, Vailima, sits in the hills above Apia and his tomb is on top of the mountain alongside. I decided to put off visiting it until I had spent more time exploring the island itself.

There was a friendly car-hire firm in town that tried harder, called me by my first name and told me that the only way to cross to the south shore would be via the cross-island road cutting the island in two. The map was not entirely to be believed. It showed roads where there weren't, and even where they were they were impassable to anything other than a four-wheel drive. No, they didn't have any four-wheel drives. The most beautiful beaches were on Upolu's southern shore.

I headed away from the town and the sea, towards the mountains on a small tarmacked curving road. From high in the hills, in the very centre of the island, I could almost have seen both shores. There were stunning views across to the southern shore and the ocean beyond. The narrow lane wound through thatched villages set behind village greens of immaculately manicured lawns. Traditional thatched fales occasionally gave way to modern tin-roofed ones, but still with the same beehive shape and still open, apart from woven blinds which could be let down for privacy or against the weather. Inside, shadowy figures raised their heads in greeting as I drove slowly through. Some of the huts were raised high on concrete bases, the height directly in proportion to the owner's status.

In front of many of the fales, in the middle of their front lawn, sat the graves and tombstones of departed ancestors, also raised. Here too, how high the tomb was raised off the ground denoted the importance of the deceased. Some of the graves were decorated with flowers, others with the occasional portrait. Some of them were quite ostentatious – Samoans obviously liked to do well by their dear departed. On one tomb, five khaki and white goats lounged seductively up the steps and slept peacefully on the stone slab at the top; on another a dog stretched out, flattened by the heat.

Apart from the heat and the extraordinary shape and layout of the villages, it might have been pre-war Surrey. Skinny horses grazed on lawns under the trees and the front gardens and village greens were elaborate with borders of stocks and busy Lizzies. Each village church held pride of place on the village green. They too were raised, some of them monumentally so. Whether it was symbolic of the villagers' generosity or an attempt to outdo one another I wasn't sure.

As I got further away from Apia and nearer to the south coast the intensity of the *Homes and Gardens* competition ceased. Fales were elevated on volcanic lava rather than cement. Village boundaries were less of a display. Taro gardens were cultivated rather than flowers, and black-eyed Susans grew wild in the roadside. On this side of the island, the villages looked considerably less well-off. They were settled under groves of trees and usually at the side of rushing streams – better for the taro. Fat pigs rooted in the undergrowth and scurried across the road nose to tail. I put up a silent prayer to Tagaloa – Samoa's God the Father – to keep it that way. No beach parks or picnic areas please, I said.

A weathered wooden signpost stuck at the side of the road pointed and said 'Return to Paradise Beach', called after the film of the same name starring Gary Cooper. I envisaged the director combing the South Seas to find the perfect beach with the perfect palms and crying '*Eureka*!' when he found it. There was no doubt it *was* magical – more as if an art director had created it rather than happened upon it. Black, shiny, volcanic boulders tumbled into the sea over the white sand. They formed boundaries around natural crystal-blue pools. The surf racing in broke on the black rocks and suddenly mellowed. The entire beach was shaded by skinny, leaning palm trees.

A chalked sign at the edge of the village whose shoreline it was asked for two tala for the use of beach and road. It was a large and prosperous-looking village. Several of the fales sported tin roofs, and a matai's meeting was taking place to discuss a new sewerage system.

A crushed-coral road led from the village for half a mile or more alongside brilliant white sand and under the dancing shadows of the palm trees. The surf thundered on to the reef, and there was wicked-looking coral everywhere. Swimming in a totally innocent opaline pool, I found I couldn't make it back to shore although I wasn't being taken anywhere – swimming yet motionless. Changing direction and circling round the rocks in an anti-clockwise direction, I finally managed to get back to shore feeling slightly stupid.

I decided to follow the lagoon back to Apia. The map I'd bought said the road existed. What's more, it was quite clearly marked in red. I set off back through the village, keeping the lagoon on my left. These were all fishing people here. A man and a little girl silhouetted against the sun stood calf-deep in the lagoon, net-fishing. The art isn't only in throwing the net so that it falls flat but also in placing yourself in the light in such a way that the fish don't see the sudden shadow of your movement as you throw. Small boys were sitting at the side of the road selling strings of smoked fish hanging from poles. It was late afternoon and the sun was turning from blinding white to purple.

About five miles on, the road slithered to a halt, right in the middle of a village between two rows of thatched huts, ending abruptly in a sheer drop. In front of me, deep down in a ravine, women and children were washing in a great rushing stream under the shade of bread-fruit trees. It was a Gauguinesque scene of extraordinary beauty, unchanged for centuries. I felt I had intruded badly, but I was too captivated by the timelessness and peacefulness of it all to want to move away. A schoolgirl appeared at my side. 'The road's very bad,' she said. 'You'll have to go back, I'm afraid.'

Children appeared from everywhere with confusing directions on the best place to turn the car, running alongside with shrieks of delight. At the end of the village, an old man waved me to a halt and asked, in the most precise English, if I could spare him a minute. He had, he said, something he'd like to show me. He led the way along a path to the back of a hut that had so much clutter in it that it looked like something from H.E. Bates' *The Darling Buds of May*. The old man himself was in a fairly dilapidated state. He wore a torn lava-lava and a filthy shirt. But his English was impeccable.

He took me to a tree-stump on the top of which someone had engineered a great metal lid. I thought it was a well at first. He lifted the lid, and inside sat one of the oddest creatures I had ever seen. It was straight out of *Alice in Wonderland* – a cross between a lobster and a crab or perhaps a turtle, a mutation of some kind. It had huge lobster pincers, but its carapace was the shape of a turtle's shell, bluish in colour. It was hard to say how big it was – possibly a couple of feet long from the pincers to the end of its shell. The old man had found it climbing a coconut palm – it loved coconut, he said. Then, wheedlingly, he said, 'It would be nice, perhaps, to take a photograph of it and send it to a scientific magazine to find out what it is.'

By now he had picked it up carefully, taken it from its cell in the tree-stump and put it on the ground. It sat with its back against a tree, waving its pincers furiously. I felt sorry for it. He gave it a saucepan of fresh water. I asked him if he'd shown it to the local fishermen; they must have known what it was. 'No,' he put his finger against his lips conspiratorially – 'I don't want to.' He extended his hand. 'Well,' he said formally, 'I mustn't keep you. Thank you so much.'

In the driving mirror I could see the old man, silhouetted against the bleached white road, his hand raised in salute until I reached the turning-off towards the tarmac road.

★

Samoa, say the writers, is 'the cradle of Polynesia'. A 'cultural storehouse', say the anthropologists. There are sixteen islands in the two Samoas – seven in American, nine in Western Samoan – but you can only find two of them on the map, smaller than pinheads and without shape. Just the names show they're there somewhere, part of the stepping-stones between Tahiti and Vanuatu, or Tonga and Fiji.

Apart from Tonga, Samoan villages are probably the last places in the Pacific where traditional Polynesian society remains intact, fiercely defended by the matai, who have most to lose by its disappearance. Fa'a Samoa – the Samoan way – is a phrase constantly used, constantly repeated. On Friday evenings and Saturday mornings, small children and adolescents spend their time clearing the fallen frangipani blossoms and leaves from the village lawns mowed to velvet perfection. This is Fa'a Samoa. In the evenings there are curfew hours and prayers. This is Fa'a Samoa. The head of the family distributes the earnings of the working members, and each family contributes to the upkeep and needs of the village – which is also their family. This too is Fa'a Samoa. To the visitor it seems as if all is as it ought to be: God's in his heaven and all's right with the world. The children are seen and not heard, and the welfare of the village takes precedence. Fa'a Samoa.

Samoans are fiercely religious. When the first missionaries arrived here, they had been spurred on to their evangelizing by the successes of the American Protestants in Hawaii. When the first of John Williams' preachers landed, they found the island split into warring factions. The Christians proved adept at playing off all sides against the middle, and within a few years Christianity had taken hold over nearly all the Samoan islands. The church's history has since been one of continuing success.

The policy of many of the missions throughout the Pacific was to use native catechists or pastors from other Pacific islands to precede the Europeans. This they did in Samoa too. For the Samoans, who had their own version of a God – Tagaloa – and heaven and hell, it was no hardship to embrace Christianity. In Lowell Holmes's observant book on life in a Samoan village,[1] he argues that the Samoans' natural love of oratory meant that they liked the sermons, which helped them along the primrose path. Many Talking Chiefs – so called for their facility with words – became substitute pastors. Besides, they had always believed in an immortal soul which, he writes, 'left the body at the time of death and went to Pulotu . . . where it never rains and where people eat and drink without labour'.

Unlike the Hawaiians, the Samoans had no idols or temples that demanded to be destroyed, although they did have to renounce polygamy, adultery, tattooing, pre-marital sex, gambling, liquor and sorcery. Christianity, however, had its advantages, and the Samoans weren't slow in realizing it:

> . . . the English people . . . have noble things while we have only canoes. They have strong beautiful clothes of various colours while we have only ti leaves . . . they have sharp knives while we have only bamboo. I, there-fore, think that the God who gave them all things must be superior to ours. If we receive God and worship Him He will, in time, give us these things as well as them.

Perhaps one of the greatest advantages of Christianity was that it could be adopted without interfering with the social structure of things: chiefs, the village council, the power system – all could remain intact. It is said, perhaps with the benefit of hindsight, that the Samoans 'Samoanized Christianity'. In return, the missionaries introduced literacy and a written language, creating the fourteen-letter Samoan alphabet.

★

Bob Barlow had recommended I meet a local historian, Feliz Va'a. It was good to find an academic actually on the island – most of them were teaching in universities overseas. We talked of the problems of retaining traditional Polynesian values.

'The main agent of change is money,' Va'a said. 'People are becoming independent. Now wealth brings "mana" – power. Now they can break away from the village control. But,' he added, 'there are limits to liberal thinking. People can be expelled by the village.'

He went on to explain 'respect behaviour', whereby children (and adults) are expected to behave respectfully and politely towards their elders, foreigners or strangers.

'Respect behaviour is typically Samoan,' Va'a said. 'The Samoans believe in group support. But Western influence is very powerful – freedom is a relative matter.'

I edged the conversation delicately round towards suicide. Samoans have the highest suicide rate in the world, and the youngest – fourteen to twenty-three-year-olds. The commonest method of suicide is by drinking a weed-killer called paraquat which is cheap and easy to get hold of. Like others before him Va'a saw suicide as a form of resistance.

'Rebellion. Why shouldn't I do what I want, meet my friends, go walking with them? Then the mother scolds the girl for letting the family down . . . guilt . . . I'm free to do what I want. If I kill myself, I've atoned for my guilt.'

'Go and see the Faolo Society,' he said. 'Translated literally it means "I want to live." ' Then he added, 'But don't forget to look at the economy; it's the key to many things.'

I wandered back down the hill to town thinking about the suicide issue, and felt oddly light-headed when I got back. I spent the next two days in bed with sunstroke.

★

A couple of days later I surfaced. A jolly Australian lady, Vicki, passing through the library suggested we spend Sunday morning not at church in the Samoan way but climbing Mount Vaea to pay homage to Robert Louis Stevenson. 'I'd prefer to do it in company,' she said.

At dawn we caught a taxi as far as Vailima, the Stevenson home. The early morning mist hung low, and people had started to light their fires. Mist and wood-smoke mingled, and it was the only time of day when the light was soft and filtering. Vailima, now State House, was unpretentious and comfortably ordinary-looking. In a hybrid colonial style, it is no longer as Stevenson built it; successive Administrations have taken it and altered it over the years. Inside, however, it still boasts the only fireplace on Samoa and a ballroom. Stevenson and his wife, Fanny, brought in everything from America or Europe or Australia and lived well here, eating oysters imported from New Zealand, drinking wines imported from France. Their servants were dressed in traditional lava-lavas, but in the Stevenson tartan. The precious piano was encased in glass to protect it from the humidity.

The Stevensons had always travelled eccentrically throughout the Pacific, taking a full entourage with them, plus his mother and Fanny's children from her first marriage, as well as hammocks, revolvers, his cigars, her seeds, his typewriter, her medicines. A journal of the day, the *Pacific Commercial Advertiser*, announced his forth-coming departure thus: 'Robert Louis Stevenson and party leave by the schooner *Equator* for the Gilbert Islands. It is to be hoped that Mr Stevenson will not fall victim to native spears, but in his state of present bodily health perhaps the temptation to kill him may not be very strong.' A reference to his crippling tuberculosis.[2]

The Stevensons arrived in Samoa in 1890 from the Marquesas, north-east of Tahiti, where Gauguin had ended his days. Stevenson bought 400 acres of ground for £1 an acre and called it Vailima – Five Streams. He got a poor bargain: only 300 of the 400 acres belonged to the original seller, and there were four streams conjoining, not five. When the family disembarked from the ship in Apia, the local clergyman thought them street entertainers, possibly because Fanny was carrying a guitar and her son a ukelele.

Apia was then rather as it is now – low, wooden clapboard buildings and plenty of churches. There must have been some sleazier haunts, because Apia was known as a kind of Pacific Sin City. Some even called it the hell of the Pacific, though it's hard today to see why.

Fanny's diaries of the time make fairly dull reading. She threw herself into gardening and growing, complaining that she was unable to find a spade or a rake in Apia, 'yet there would be no difficulty in finding the best quality champagne.'

Stevenson's perceptions were different, and it is his humour and descriptiveness that lifts their accounts of life in Samoa on to another plane. 'The natives walk in a foreign town,' he wrote. Apia was, he said, 'a place administered by whites, for whites, and the whites themselves holding it not in common, but in hostile camps so that it lies between them like a bone between two dogs . . .'

Vicki and I hiked along a dirt path alongside the house, walking on carpets of blossoms that had dropped from high above, tree hibiscus six inches across, a glorious peach colour with deep-purple centres. The rain-forest was so dense you couldn't see the sky through the canopy of branches. The ocean seemed almost non-existent now, with only the enveloping rain-forest all round with its tree-ferns and orchids. The climb was steep and muddy. As we arrived at the top of the mountain, shafts of sunlight and blue sky broke through the branches. A small woven shelter had been put there for travellers. Mount Vaea isn't a very big mountain, but we felt we were at the top of the world. Stevenson had certainly picked his spot. To the west lay the ocean, and somewhere down there, through the haze, Apia itself. To the east were rolling green hills, rain-forest-covered mountains and, immediately below, a fertile valley and the sprawling tin roof of Vailima.

I sat on a ledge on Stevenson's tomb looking out at the mountains and the ocean and read the words so familiar from my schooldays:

> Under the wide and starry sky,
> Dig my grave and let me lie.
> Glad did I live and gladly die,
> And I laid me down with a will.
>
> This be the verse you grave for me:
> *Here he lies where he longed to be;*
> *Home is the sailor, home from the sea,*
> *And the hunter home from the hill.*

It was strange to see the words in their rightful setting. A quiet calm surrounded the place, and I was sure that benevolent aitu – spirits – must be there.

The Road of the Loving Heart was the name given to the route up the side of Mount Vaea. Story has it that, upon Stevenson's death, heart-broken natives hacked their way through the forest to the top of the mountain and carried his coffin up, but this is not entirely true. The truth is more complicated.

Although it was a small island a long way away, Samoa went through the latter years of the nineteenth century being buffeted by extraordinary and complex politickings and schemings by the then great superpowers: America, Great Britain and Germany. The three powers were not so much interested in making further gains in Samoa – they had those already via missions, trading companies and plantations – they were more interested in keeping everybody else out. The Samoan leaders, too, had been warring among themselves for years. Finally, during the years of the Berlin Conference, when the European powers were consolidating their hold on their colonial possessions, they were able to reach agreement that Samoan political structures should be re-organized and that the Samoans be allowed independence and the right to elect their own king and government. There was, however, one small oversight. Nobody had thought to establish any kind of electoral procedure. Chaos and civil war broke out with various claimants to the kingship. The three great powers each backed their own man and then Germany sneakily hoisted the flag and declared war on one of the Samoan kings. They all sent warships, Germany and the United States three each and Great Britain one. Fortunately, as they at squaring up to each other in tiny Apia harbour, a typhoon broke, hitting them before they could unleash their gunpowder on each other or the island.

It took a Joint Commission to eventually sort out the mess and get everyone to surrender their arms. The Americans got Pago Pago harbour on Tutuila; the Germans got Western Samoa and renounced their claims to various other Pacific islands in favour of the British.

Throughout, Stevenson had been deeply involved in these events and wrote a series of letters to *The Times* and to the Foreign Office. He had identified himself with one of the claimants to the kingship, Mataafa, leader of the anti-German faction. After Mataafa's arrest by the Germans, Stevenson, well aware of the effects of imprisonment upon Polynesians, had continued to visit the leader and his followers in jail and had continued to plead their case to the British. It was these Samoans and their clansmen who eventually built the Road of the Loving Heart and, out of loyalty to Stevenson and Fanny, carried his coffin up through the rain-forest above Vailima to its resting place at the top of the mountain.

At the foot of Mount Vaea we splashed in the streams he loved so much. It was still early, and walking back into Apia we passed families on their way to church, wearing large picture hats and dressed from head to foot in white. They greeted us politely. Respectability behaviour.

★

I was still finding it hard to relate the outward and visible signs of this glorious tropical island to the obvious pressures that its communal village life was presenting to generations of young Samoans.

Albert Wendt's *Leaves of the Banyan Tree* was making depressing reading. Wendt cast an entirely different and cynical light on both the matai system and the pressures of the extended family, something that most Westerners have always romanticized. A novel, his book is a study of three generations and the effects on individual, village and family life that financial success and social status bring about. I was dismayed by his anger, fascinated by his perspective.

'Fa'a Samoa,' said Gabriel, a teacher from New Zealand – 'that can mean many things.' She layered bread-fruit into a baking dish for supper. 'It's a very closed society here – hard to get under the surface. And things are changing. A friend of mine had an accident the other day and broke her leg. As she was being carried to the side of the road, she was robbed.' She looked at me with a beady eye. 'There are problems, whatever people say. Don't walk out after sunset and don't *ever* take a taxi late at night – there have been incidents.'

'What kind of incidents?'

'Pack rape.'

'I thought that was a Papua New Guinea phenomenon. How long have you been here?' I asked.

'About four months,' she said. 'They say if you get past four weeks then you'll probably stay.'

The bus to Gabriel's school had dropped me at a village just outside the town. Elaborate displays of hibiscus and frangipani threaded together along the tops of the village walls signalled a women's committee meeting the next day. I walked up a narrow dirt road bordering the village green towards the school. Old men sat outside their huts taking in the last minutes of sunset.

Gabriel's house in the school grounds was under a great bread-fruit tree. There were several teachers there, including a tall, dark, edgy Scandinavian.

'There's a lot of emphasis on education and the urge to

succeed,' said Gabriel. 'There are girls and boys here in their twenties who are in the fifth form.'

'Isn't there pressure on them to leave school and start work?'

'No,' she said, 'because they'll go to university and they'll go overseas and they'll remit money.'

'So the pressure is a different one: that they do well in school and go on to university?'

'Education,' one of the older teachers explained, 'is everything. Samoa is classified as an LDC – a Least Developed Country. Both the island and each aiga are economically dependent on money remitted from relatives abroad. The brain drain.'

The Scandinavian girl seemed strung-out and nervous. 'It's oppressive here,' she said – 'the public humiliation, the beatings at school. I teach at a boys school, and you should see the national teachers, not the Europeans. They use rubber hoses. And encourage the other pupils to hit them. I come from Norway, where we don't have any corporal or capital punishment. I'm an educational psychologist.'

'Here, children are beaten at quite a small age,' said Gabriel – 'certainly in the village, at home. Maybe it's the pressures of other kids. Maybe it's when they get to beyond toddler stage, but they're still quite small.'

One of the older teachers said abruptly, 'Fa'a Samoa – it's like a spider's web in its complexity and its supporting seams and cross-threads. It is beautiful, intricate and lethal.' She laughed and said, 'And in this society it goes vertical as well.'

'A society of double standards,' said the Norwegian. The other teachers were not in disagreement. It was the third time I had heard those words that day.

★

I thought it was finally time that I visited the Faolo Clinic. Sister Barbara there was keen that I talk to her local counterpart, Katy. Katy had been trained as a nurse in

New Zealand. She had been there for fourteen years and had been back in Samoa for eight months. Gently she tried to explain to me the nightmares attached to preserving a traditional Polynesian society.

'In traditional Fa'a Samoa, everyone had an identity. The lowest servant knew who he was. That was eroded, mainly by the European influences coming in and, of course, migration. The mind-set is still set on traditional values, but in reality they've gone. The real meaning of extended family is that everyone is responsible for everybody else. But now people are not part of the older matai system nor part of the Western system. There is an immense wall between old and young generations,' she said.

'Hence the high suicide rate?'

'They don't kill themselves because of failure,' explained Sister Barbara, 'but because of the threatened destruction of a cherished relationship.'

'I am counselling a forty-year-old woman', said Katy softly, 'who supports fifteen people in her family. She sits down at the end of the week and gives her salary to her father, who hands out so many tala for you, so many tala for you.' Katy dealt an invisible pack of cards. 'Now she's had to take out a loan to contribute towards a wedding.

'The expectations are to obey your parents until they die, and if you don't there are beatings galore. People feel oppressed, particularly those at the bottom of the social and economic heap. That', she said leaning forward, 'is the crushingness of the matai system.'

The Government doesn't release information on the numbers of matai titles held, but they're probably double what they were. Often titles are split in an effort to resolve a controversy, but several title-holders can mean conflicts in residual rights over land. The rigid social structures of the matai system create frustration.

'In Fa'a Samoa, personal relationships are more important than wealth or individual achievements, but at the same time there are social commitments that encourage people to live beyond their means and they simply can't cope economically. It is better to die than to live in shame,' said Katy. 'Many of the victims come from families that are socially isolated and, because of this, lack stability. There is the inability to cope with unexpressed feelings.'

Katy had an enviable mixture of gentleness and immense firmness. In New Zealand, as part of her training, she had done a self-awareness programme. 'I was very subservient before I went away,' she said with a sweet smile.

'When we're children, we become assets. That's how children are looked upon, as assets.

'You know, recently I came across an eight-year-old child left to look after an old lady. The family had left the village.' She lit a cigarette. 'There are many cases of old people living alone. Their families are in New Zealand. Their families put them into old-people's homes and never go near them again.'

'But Pacific societies are the home of the extended family. It's against all the mores of the society.'

Katy looked at me through large, slanting brown eyes. 'Look, I'm now thirty-six and I have only just now developed a relationship with my mother. Do you know, I don't recall her ever saying to me she loved me or giving me a hug. There's no bonding between mother and child. There's bonding within the extended family, to other kids who are coming along, but usually there are about twelve other kids in the family. The women have no time. There's the women's committee, the church functions – these take their energy away from their family and child. In the evenings you sit in and sing hymns and say prayers, and that's it.

'For the men it's a different story. Men's virility is shown by kids – so if you can't give them any more they'll go out and have one by another woman. But a girl's still got to be a virgin.' She crossed one forefinger over the other. 'On the other hand, boys have to make a list of girls. Male virility has to be maintained. At a woman's menopause, a man will often leave her for a younger woman. There is no consideration of how she might need fulfilment or sexual satisfaction.'

I told her of Papua New Guinea women and how I had wondered if the sins of the colonizers had been visited upon the colonized. She listened, then told me that New Zealand, like Australia, has a horrendous record of wife abuse, alcohol abuse and growing violent crime. 'In the professional classes especially,' said Katy – 'doctors, for example, who know where to damage, and where it won't show.'

New Zealand had been the administrator of Western Samoa before independence.

I walked slowly along Beach road and round the curve of the bay. Apia was taking on the dimensions of a large town and seemed suddenly as unappealing. It was sounding all as Wendt had written. But why should I be surprised to find the island unable to escape these impacts? No society can remain static. Perhaps I too had fallen into the trap of searching for the last earthly paradise and was disappointed that it wasn't here.

I waded knee-deep through dead coral out towards the reef, to a wooden platform raised on wooden piles on the edge of a deep. Someone had built a thatched roof on the end of the platform for shade, and you could sit out in the middle of the ocean, cooled by the breeze, and listen to the surf crashing on the reef. Upolu looked like a true paradise from here. Below, in the deep, the coral was the size of table-tops. Schools of garfish drifted by like silver leaves.

A masked New Zealander surfaced from the coral, a hat pulled over his ears, held in place by the rubber straps of the snorkel. He climbed the spindly ladder to the platform and, as we sat in the sun, he told me of some Americans who had arrived on the island with a plan for recycling fuel oil. They'd tried it on Tonga first, then Samoa. Their plan was to persuade the Government to allow them to build a plant for recycling the waste chemicals that are left from the refining of fuel oils – a difficult, dirty and at times dangerous business. Quite rightly, the Samoans had deported them as undesirable aliens.

The New Zealander worked for the Health Department and was familiar with what he called 'the epidemic of suicide by paraquat'. 'One mouthful can be fatal,' he said, 'and what might be perceived as a gesture by the victim unwittingly turns out to be fatal. In fairness to ICI they're well aware of the problem and now distribute a detoxifier pack – fuller's earth usually – but Western Samoa is an agricultural society and no suitable alternative to paraquat has yet been identified. It's cheap and efficient.

'You have to realize,' he said, 'in these countries there are no laws regarding the labelling, sale or distribution of pesticides. Often it's decanted into unlabelled containers – beer bottles, soft-drinks bottles. How do you enforce the law even if you do draw up legislation? And if Western Samoa reduced the use of paraquat, who's to say they wouldn't find another way?'

He promised to drop by a South Pacific Commission report, definite in its conclusions: the precipitating event was invariably something that Westerners would consider minor – a scolding or a rebuke. 'A cry from the powerless' was how they put it.

Other Pacific islands were experiencing the same problem, particularly in Micronesia. The breakdown of traditional rituals and roles during young men's transition from adolescence to manhood left them with no recognized role, in a vacuum and more dependent on their parents.

★

'Perhaps the family is too strong,' said the Reverend Amosa Vaetoe. He was a big man and spoke haltingly, unsure of his English. As Director of Education for the Congregational Christian Church, the Rev. Vaetoe was responsible for youth activities in the Church. 'Samoan society is still conservative,' he said. 'The parents teach them through scolding and beating. They try to remind the young of what they should be.

'So many changes have come in – with tourism, with migration. Some youngsters look upon town as the answer to their needs – happiness, freedom, an easy life. They yearn to come to town; they identify town with money; they identify the white people with money.'

He lit a cigarette and slowly drew on it. 'I think one of the problems from the Church itself . . .', he paused, 'is the gap between young and old. The Church is not fully committed towards the young.'

'I was born on Savaii,' he said. 'I was brought up on a plantation. We didn't see another world. It's not like the palagi – Europeans – where they're free at 21 to do what they want. I didn't ever dream I could get a car.'

'Samoan society is still conservative,' he said, 'They are responsible to the matai. However mature you are, that's your responsibility, until you die.'

Then he leaned back in his chair and used those words again: 'All of us are the children of our parents. We're treasure. We were brought up in that kind of life-style. Then why not today? It's the impact of education. We only offer the kind of education that deals with commercial, administrative things. It doesn't apply to the villages. Computers,' he said sighing – 'we can't find computers in the villages, so why not change our education system? Education is a way of colouring the mind of a person. People dream for their children to have white-collar jobs,' he said sadly. 'White-collar jobs are the answer to their dreams. How to educate and apply it within our own situation?' He lit another cigarette, leaving the question unanswered. Outside the Rev. Vaetoe's window a haze of heat was building up over the black-green rain-forest of Mount Vaea.

★

Back at Aggies I found a Christmas parcel on my bed, with

fir trees, glass balls and Santas stamped all over it. It was folded over and neatly stapled down like a giant envelope. When I opened it, my laundry was inside.

In the bar, a tall young Australian, recently arrived, was telling the story of how he had been idly flicking through a filing-cabinet in his office when he discovered a number of files – seventeen, to be precise. From them he realized that seventeen people had preceded him to Apia to do the job that he was now contracted to do. 'Seventeen,' he said, 'over as many years. They were certainly as well qualified as I am. And some of them . . .' he paused for emphasis, 'some of them were even better qualified. So I got to asking myself, what is it about this place that none of them succeeded in getting it right?'

'Have another drink mate,' said a sympathetic Englishman, who was also there on contract, to put in a new telephone system.

The contract workers are the new cowboys of the Pacific. They are today what the prospectors and trade-store owners were in the twenties and thirties. For them the islands are a global village and rated by the price of the beer, the attraction and availability of the women and the Westernisation of the food.

The Australian was continuing with another story. 'It's all happened before,' he said. 'The jumpers aren't connected by day but at night. The phantom subscribers come on the line, they make international calls – except they aren't subscribers.' He was exasperated. 'My job is to try and audit the number into which the jumpers are connected. The numbers exist, but there is no subscriber. Do you know, if you don't pay your bill here, after three months they just stop sending them to you.' He grinned and raised his eyebrows, then raised his glass of beer. 'Fa'a Samoa.'

We filed out to Otto's Reef to carry on drinking. The barman put a frangipani lei over my head as he took our orders. The Australian continued his saga of Fa'a Samoa. He pointed to a pot-bellied European playing darts. 'See that chap over there? He's on a contract as an agricultural advisor on taro.'

'But they've been growing it for two thousand years.'

'I know,' he said. 'See what I mean?'

The scams didn't end there. Had I seen, he asked, the two men drinking at the side of Aggie's pool. I hadn't. 'They're here on a grant from the Smithsonian, touring the Pacific, warning island governments about the brown snake.'

'You have to be joking! Samoa doesn't have any snakes. The brown snake lives on Guam.'

There were a series of stories as to how the brown snake had arrived on Guam in the first place. Some say it was introduced from the Philippines after the war; others that it stowed away on cargo ships from the Solomons. Either way it has since caused a lot of environmental damage. Harmless to humans it might be; unfortunately it is harmful to everything else – birds' eggs, local lizards, flora, fauna. The brown snake had decimated Guam's local bird population and had now added chickens to its diet. Stories abound of the resourcefulness and cheek of the snake – every time you opened a cupboard door, you could expect to find one smiling at you, having first eaten its way through the contents, of course. They had even been blamed for power failures and interference with electrical installations.

'Well, whether you like it or not, those guys are on a grant to travel the Pacific for the next year . . .'

'But Guam is thousands of miles away from here. How are the snakes going to get here? Swim?'

'Wheels,' said my drinking companion.

'Wheels?'

'They get into the undercarriages of planes.'

'But there are no planes flying between here and Guam. Continental flies to Guam; it doesn't fly here. And you'd have to go via Hawaii or PNG. It's not a million miles away, but it might as well be.'

'Well,' said John, 'that's what they told me, and that's

why they've got this grant.'

'Are they seriously suggesting that the snake is bright enough to catch a Continental flight to Hawaii, change terminals and get on the once-a-week flight to Apia, which comes in via Pago Pago. That it will have the sense not to disembark at Pago but will carry on till it reaches here?'

'Well, why don't you talk to them?' said John.

'I will,' I said.

But the next day the two men had left the island to continue their awareness campaign.

★

One day a New Zealander with a long moustache and a lugubrious look drifted into Aggies. He drank there in the evenings, taking off to sleep in one of the cheaper guest-houses further round the bay. He spent much of his time sitting mournfully on the wooden bench outside the hotel. He had, he said, once worked on contract in American Samoa and was trying to recapture some of the magic of that time. Somehow it wasn't working out right.

I saw him one morning, sitting on a wooden bench under the palm trees, gazing out across the bay.

'How's it going?'

'Terrible,' he said.

He had, it seemed, agreed to help a New Zealand girls' netball team tour the island. The girls said that they had arranged it all beforehand but a few of the arrangements needed finalizing – dates, for example. Brendan had visited a fair number of schools and colleges on the island, only to discover that none of them had netball pitches or even nets. Worse still, they knew nothing of any tour. Now the girls had arrived. No one had been expecting them, and the village where he had arranged for them to stay had, for some unaccountable reason, gone walkabout. In the early hours of the morning he had managed to find a smaller, poorer village for them to stay in, but it was a strain on the resources of the one side and on the patience of the other. There were fifteen girls, plus chaperones, all in one room, all sharing one toilet and one shower. He was trying to help them move to another village today.

'To tell you the truth,' said Brendan bitterly, 'I don't think they could arrange to open a brown envelope.'

The idea of fifteen boisterous schoolgirls out to have a good time, netball or not, was too much for him, let alone the island boys.

'Know what I think?' asked Brendan. 'I reckon we've really stuffed these islands,' he said with passion. 'They'd be better if we'd left them alone and never been here.'

The newly installed main Apia switchboard was to be celebrated with an umu – a traditional feast. There was to be roast pig and palusami – taro leaves stuffed with coconut cream. It was a blisteringly hot Saturday, and my initial enthusiasm was wavering. The underground oven had been started some hours earlier in somebody's back garden. Politeness demanded I go. In a room at the back of the stark, modern building, almost empty of furniture, four little Japanese sat lined up together on a sofa. They were aid workers, here to ensure the smooth running of the new switchboard. There was a keg of beer sitting in a red plastic bowl of ice. We'd all drunk too much by the time the pig arrived, with a hibiscus in its mouth. The matai, who were supposed to arrive at the same time as the pig, had been delayed by a traffic accident, which presented a protocol problem – to eat or not to eat? Officially there was no way we should eat before the matai arrived. One of the Japanese lurched outside. 'I'm so drunk,' he wailed unhappily. 'In Japan we eat and drink at the same time.' We tried to stay sober and exchanged politenesses about places visited and languages spoken. They took advantage of the delay to ask about the correct usages of English grammar. 'Please,' said one. ' "I must go" or "I have to go". Which is correct, please?'

We were more than slightly tiddly by the time the matai arrived. The pig was ceremoniously carved on to paper plates. One of the Japanese sidled up. He was carefully stowing bits of food into a large plastic bag. 'That's very tidy,' I said. He smiled and put his hand up to the side of his mouth so that the matai wouldn't hear. 'It's for my cat,' he whispered.

★

Two days later, a smiling golden imp arrived in town. He was almost single-handedly sailing a ketch to Nouméa. I christened him the Larrikin, as he had a cheeky smile and a sharp wit – although, after several months, the strains of shipboard life were beginning to tell. He told me how one crew member had already abandoned ship and was repatriated home at the owner's expense. It pays to choose your crew well and your skippers too. The worst owners, the Larrikin had decided, were those who fly in for the day, sip champagne under the canopy, swop stories with the other owners and then fly out again.

One day he invited me aboard. He had adapted a piece of hibiscus lava-lava into a kind of turban, tied at the back with cord, which he wore against the sun. It gave him a kind of piratical look. In between gossip, we occasionally fell overboard into the black waters of the bay to cool off. No sound from the shore reached us. A school of large fish broke the surface of the bay. They rose and fell like an aquatic merry-go-round, shimmering silver against the light, changing direction again as a small, elegant black-timbered yacht sailed across to the wharf – a lone Swede. 'Christ,' said the Larrikin, 'you have to have a lot of guts to go it alone. I've had a look over his boat. It's not in great shape but, I tell you something, I'd rather be crossing the Pacific in that any day.'

The problem with the Larrikin's trip was that it had lacked a certain democracy. He had volunteered for the crewing job, taking six months off work in order to see the Pacific. The skipper's girlfriend was on board and ran a tight ship. Mutiny was in the air after she had taken a violent dislike to the crew kicking their heels when they hit land for a few days. I remarked that the skipper had seemed a bit of a cold fish.

'Cold fish!' said the Larrikin. 'He's an arrogant bastard, that's what he is. And to think I was at school with him! He used to be one of me mates!'

Apia, the Larrikin decided, was a great place for travellers – not tourists, he declared, but travellers. It had the quality of a time before, when traders and whalers and entrepreneurs passed through. A good place for meeting drifters. Which was how we befriended Scobie. He was travelling the South Pacific doing a little soul-searching on his way to Tahiti, and after that who knows where? Among the spivs and carpetbaggers of Aggie's bar, Scobie stood out as something of a sophisticated and cultured man. He was particularly fond of the Polynesians. He had had a long time of doing the same job in the same place, married to the same woman, carrying out the same routine. Free of all of them now, he had a strong need to socialize. And socialize we did.

Both he and the Larrikin had the quality of curiosity. Every outing became a voyage of discovery. We trekked round a series of bars, discovering a large-gutted German, a lisping Spaniard, a timid yachtie from Maine, an American Samoan woman running a slightly seedy bar on the edges of Apia. With a disarming handshake, the two of them would introduce themselves to anyone and everyone. A practising Christian, Scobie went to church the next day to do penance, but his remorse didn't last long. His love for his fellow-man would take hold again, his positive joy in the Samoans would re-emerge and he would head off the next day with the Larrikin in one hand and me in the other looking for the next adventure.

The day he took off in his yacht, we stood at the foot of the steps until she vanished over the horizon. 'Come on, old girl,' said the Larrikin, sensing my sadness at seeing him go, 'I'll buy you a beer.' But the sparkle had gone, and the two of us on our own were no match for Scobie.

Not long after, the Larrikin left too. The morning he

sailed, he asked me to take his photograph with a couple of the pretty Samoan bar girls at Aggies. I walked with him to the dinghy moored at the bottom of the steps. 'Sorry to leave Apia,' he said. 'Best place yet, old girl. Best place yet.' At the bottom of the steps he pushed a postcard into my hand. It was of an old four-masted schooner. On the back he had written a note thanking me for my company. Then he gave me a smacking kiss, clambered into the dinghy and roared off across the bay. I felt I'd lost two of my best friends.

I walked into town to the Australian High Commission, to read its wire service. There was a transcript of an ABC radio broadcast announcing that, in Palau, President Lazarus Salii had been found dead in his house with a bullet through his head. A verdict of suicide was expected. In Papua New Guinea the Government had been forced to step down, but the Prime Minister had refused to leave Government House and the police had had to remove him.

It was a full moon when I left Apia, just as it had been when I arrived. On the bus to the airport we passed a sugar-pink and green concoction of a house, neon lighting surrealistically reflected on the surface of the lagoon like a cassata ice-cream.

Chapter 6

AMERICAN SAMOA

ROADS TO NOWHERE

As the Pacific goes, American Samoa is just a hop away from Apia, eighty miles. Socially and culturally it could be a thousand miles away or as many light-years. In Hawaii I had met a courteous, old-worldy American, Bob Allen, and his partner, Rayner Kinney, who had poured coffee and coconut cookies into me and explained their belief and their hopes that the Pacific would develop as a major tourist region. Bob enthusiastically described Pago Pago as one of the last vestiges of the old South Pacific. They had taken over the old Rainmaker Hotel there and insisted I stay as their guest, '. . . no matter what kind of book you're doing,' said Bob. It was a nice gesture.

Against the night sky, the mountain of Tutuila – American Samoa's main island – loomed black and threatening. It was a dreary night to arrive in a new place. A howling wind whipped the leaves off the palms, and on the way from the tiny airport waves broke right across the road. It was comforting to know I had a bed waiting.

Sunday dawned just as wet and just as dreary. Pago seemed to emit as much charm as Yarmouth on a wet winter's weekend. On a small crescent beach outside my room, a crew-cut American and a dark-skinned man with a pigtail worked through a slow and steady exercise routine that had neither grace or urgency. I drummed my fingers and wished I had an umbrella before deciding to call a contact of Bob's. The pretty girl in reception heaved a sigh when I asked if there was a telephone directory. She moved at a snail's pace – except for her jaws, which masticated gum feverishly. She came back after ten minutes or so and announced pleasantly, 'No book.'

'How do you make a call?'

She shrugged and moved away.

From a small room off the reception area came a kind of chanting. There was a sign on the door announcing the English Congregation Church. 'God is here to *help* you,' boomed a voice from within. The preacher sounded exasperated. 'He is *love*,' he screamed. There was a moan from the congregation. Poor Sadie Thompson, I thought, and crept back to my room.

The hotel sat on the edge of Pago's magnificent harbour, looking directly across to its namesake, Mount Pioa – Rainmaker Mountain. I knew the mountain was there somewhere, but I couldn't see it. Until now, fine drizzle had swept from north to south, bringing with it cloud and mist. Then it changed direction and moved east to west. Grey waves whirled across the mouth of the harbour. The noise of the wind crescendoed into an ear-splitting wail, and lashing rain blew straight off the sea. I moped and experienced the novelty of watching the Emmy awards on TV while munching on a pineapple.

Monday was greyer and even wetter. I didn't believe it possible – even Papua New Guinea's wet seasons and wettest places usually manage to log up a few hours of sunshine each day, the rains coming regularly enough to set your watch by. Braving the weather, I wandered into town to find a bookshop.

Pago reeked of inertia: it seeped out of every pore of every person and every place. The whole place lacked vitality – even the market-place. America had left its mark, however. There were super-marts, mini-marts, kwik-marts. The American flag flew proudly over 'The only American soil below the equator', and armed police cruised the tiny main street in a blue and white patrol car. Over everything hung the stench of the Starkist cannery.

The Starkist tentacles spread all over the Pacific. In Pago, the Starkist cannery is the second largest employer on the island, but, because American Samoans couldn't adapt to working in a fish cannery any better than their Polynesian forefathers could adapt to working on sugar plantations, or perhaps because of the lure of welfare, it is operated by Koreans and Tongans and Western Samoans, needing the work and the money.

Entitled to residency in and unrestricted entry to the United States, the American Samoans have joined the same exodus as their Micronesian cousins, migrating to Hawaii and the American mainland. The exportation of human resources has become the growth industry of the Pacific. I passed a US Army recruitment centre in a shopping arcade in downtown Pago. A queue of young men sat waiting to be interviewed. The idea of them being exported to serve in Central America or even Germany seemed both absurd and too sad for words.

American Samoa is described as 'an unorganized and unincorporated territory' of the United States. Not incorporated into the US as a state, it doesn't have access to the US court system and US law does not apply automatically. American Samoans are US nationals but not US citizens.

In 1964 America introduced a multi-million-dollar educational policy into the island: there was to be education by television. Ten years later the scheme was dead as a dodo, with the only direct result a massive rise in small businesses selling TVs and videos. Today, Tutuila can boast one hundred per cent importation of goods – shoes from Korea, T-shirts from Taiwan, booze from the States, canned pineapples from Hawaii. The main employer, needless to say, is the Government.

I rented a car that had seen better days and decided not to let the dreariness of the weather or of Pago get me down. One thing the Americans must have done was to leave paved roads, and Tutuila was a small island.

They had left roads but the scene was very different from flower-bedecked Upolu. Although the layout of the villages was similar, there were no village greens, thatched fales or velvet lawns. There was litter everywhere, and village signs had been spray-painted over by graffiti artists. There were fire-hydrants and fales with corrugated-iron roofs painted red, white and blue. Beehive fales had been replaced by concrete and tin and louvred windows. Alongside were square, Queensland-style houses, neo-tropical in vivid colours, turquoise and *eau-de-Nil* and pink.

The further I travelled, the fewer people I saw. There were no women nursing babies, no pigs rooting in the gardens. But then, I realized, there were no gardens. Outside village houses were heaps of cans – Coke, Sprite, Budweiser. Dogs had dragged the garbage out and over the road. A sign nailed on to a tree announced that the fine for littering was $100. Outside some of the decrepit-looking houses sat Chryslers, Dodges and Plymouths; Broncos, Cherokees and Cobras. There were no fishermen and no farmers. There were no young people. I saw two taro patches on the entire seventy-seven square miles of the island. It was as though I had come to a deserted island, finding only the remnants of people's lives, rusted cans and bicycles. The road stopped somewhere in a village by the sea. There wasn't a canoe or a fishing-net anywhere to be seen. A large truck was unloading cans of Coca-Cola and beer, and some stringy chickens rooted in the gravel and aggregate that substituted for a village lawn.

Depressed, I drove slowly back to the hotel. It was packed with Filipinos and Koreans. They had a strange uniformity. On their feet they wore moon-boots, puffed and padded round the ankles, the laces undone, the tongues sticking up and out. On their heads they wore baseball caps. They took on a single, amorphous yet American identity. In common with their uniform look they shared the continual motion of chewing. They could well have come from the Marshalls, the Carolines, Hawaii or southern California.

I picked up the *Samoa News* and went to Sadie's Bar where the storm was still beating off the sea. There was a story filed from Honolulu. The headlines screamed at me: 'Brown Tree Snake a Big Menace on Guam'. The Governor of Guam, said the story, was asking the US Department of Agriculture to declare the snakes a pest so that Guam would be eligible for more money to figure out how to get rid of them. The Governor was asking for $2 million of federal funding, then he would decide how to get rid of them. It seemed an odd way to go about things.

Outside the window it was no longer possible to make out the shapes of the mountains. The sea was grey and foaming white. It smashed against black volcanic rocks. I thought of Scobie sailing somewhere towards Tahiti and the Larrikin on his way to Nouméa, and I thought of Brendan's words that the islands had been stuffed. In Tutuila's case, raped.

A large Samoan girl came in to the bar. She was striking-looking and wore sneakers and tight, hibiscus-patterned Bermuda shorts that extended to the knee. She chewed mindlessly. She smiled and sat down next to me. Suddenly her lips parted. I waited for her words. Instead, she expelled a vast, pink translucent bubble, let it explode, then sucked it back in again with a happy smile. It was definitely time to go home.

NOTES

INTRODUCTION

1.   Alan Moorehead's book, *The Fatal Impact* (reissued by Hamish Hamilton 1987) covers Cook's journeys to Australia and exploration of the Antarctic, as well as Tahiti. In the book, Moorehead examines the toll exacted from the islanders by their contact with the Europeans. The book takes largely from Cook's own journals and his awareness of the repercussions that the expedition would have: massive drop in populations, creation of a money culture, syphilis, etc. Moorehead also points out that, in the case of Tahiti, Cook was preceded by both Bougainville and Wallis – who both blamed each other for the introduction of VD to the islands: '. . . certainly many of Cook's men were down with the disease within a few weeks of going ashore.'

CHAPTER 1

1.   The Dutch had never formally administered West Papua and at the time of Indonesian independence in 1949, Dutch New Guinea was not part of the independence treaty. The Dutch maintained that they were hanging on to the territory out of sympathy for the West Papuans and their claim for self-determination; Indonesia argued that the territory was part of the Dutch East Indies and rightly belonged to them. In 1962 the two sides finally got together at the UN and signed the New York Agreement which transferred Dutch New Guinea to Indonesia. The Agreement guaranteed that after six years there would be an 'Act of Free Choice', meant to give the Papuans a voice in self-determination. In 1964, however, Sukarno took Indonesia out of the UN and announced that there would be no Act of Free Choice because all the people of West Irian were in favour of being part of the Indonesian Republic. His successor, President Suharto, rescinded Sukarno's decision and re-instated the Act of Free Choice but the ensuing vote-rigging shenanigans,who could vote and who couldn't, was described as a 'fiasco'. Even so, West Papua or Irian Jaya, as it is now known, was declared to have 'chosen' to go with Indonesia.

CHAPTER 2

1.   In 1982 the Greenpeace ship, *Rainbow Warrior*, was blown up in Auckland Harbour prior to leaving for the French nuclear testing zone of Moruroa Atoll. A photographer on board was killed. It was later revealed that the French Secret Service had carried out the attack. Two French agents were charged and sent to serve out their sentence on a Pacific island. Within two

years they were released, he on the grounds of ill health, she because she became pregnant, but both on the understanding they would return after their respective 'confinements'. They still have not returned and it is once again before the UN.

CHAPTER 3

1. King Kalakaua's new constitution of 1887, admittedly forced upon him by the white planters, effectively disenfranchised native Hawaiians from government because they simply did not earn sufficient income to qualify either for voting rights or to sit in the upper house, the House of Nobles. He also signed away to the legislature his right of veto, which until then had been absolute. The number of seats in the House of Representatives was reduced to such a degree that the upper house now constituted a majority; those with property could outvote the House of Representatives, meant to represent the interests of the people. There was a feeble attempt to put Kalakaua's sister, Liliuokalani, on the throne in his place but this was foiled and the American marines were sent in instead. When Liliuokalani did accede, she attempted to drive through a new constitution which would restore royal control over the upper house and ensure that native Hawaiians enjoyed universal suffrage. Although the Hawaiian Supreme Court supported her, the Americans again threatened to send in the marines unless she agreed to modify her constitution. Hawaii's annexation had pretty well taken place, in fact if not in name.

CHAPTER 4

1. Zeder did very nicely thank you with the advent of the Bush administration. He was made Director of something called the Overseas Private Investment Corporation, an outfit that receives a mixture of federal and private funding for loans to small businesses all over the world. As a Washington friend put it: 'Now he can go round creating all sorts of mini Palaus all over the Pacific.' OPIC certainly has links to one not-so-former CIA operative who was deeply involved in the Iran-Contra affair as well as being the beneficiary of OPIC funding.

2. Nauru's wealth (the annual per capita income of the Nauruans is probably the highest in the world) is due to guano (phosphate). The phosphate mining has taken its environmental toll, however, almost turning the island into one great opencast mine.

CHAPTER 5

1. Lowell D. Holmes, *Samoan Village: Case Studies in Cultural Anthropology* (Holt, Rinehart, Winslow).

2. Stevenson in fact died of a brain haemorrhage in Samoa in 1894, four years after he arrived on the island.